YOU PACKED THE CAT
IN THE SUITCASE?!

You Gotta Get Organized

Other Books by Albert Vorspan

MY RABBI DOESN'T MAKE HOUSE CALLS
SO THE KIDS ARE REVOLTING . . . ?
MAZEL TOV! YOU'RE MIDDLE-AGED
I'M OK, YOU'RE A PAIN IN THE NECK

ALBERT VORSPAN

YOU PACKED THE CAT IN THE SUITCASE?!
You Gotta Get Organized

DOUBLEDAY AND COMPANY, INC.
GARDEN CITY, NEW YORK
1978

817
V

ISBN 0-385-12401-5
Library of Congress Catalog Card Number 77–80916
Copyright © 1978 by Albert Vorspan
ALL RIGHTS RESERVED
PRINTED IN THE UNITED STATES OF AMERICA
FIRST EDITION

103167
c. 2

CONTENTS

PROLOGUE

When the Train Pulls Out,
Don't Be Left at the Station

In a world of chaos and kaleidoscopic velocity, you'll be swept away if you aren't nailed down. You need an anchor to windward; otherwise, you'll be living your life like a frantic *tummeler* on the deck of the *Titanic*. To keep your feet on the ground, you have to be well organized. It also helps if you have a sharp eye for change, a thick skin against criticism and hemorrhoids so you'll always look concerned.

Disorganized people are always left at the station when the train pulls out. They also lose their glasses, their wallets and purses, their train tickets and their friends. They forget in which parking lot they placed their cars and miss the boat to self-fulfillment.

One overarching rule for getting organized: SLOW DOWN! Not to sweat so much. Frantic rushing means missed signs, twisted ankles, fender benders and high blood pressure, not to mention a lifetime of wheel spinning.

So get yourself organized pronto or your entire life will be a busted play!

"The mind," said St. Theresa, a fifteenth-century Spanish mystic, "is an unbroken horse." This slim volume by a twentieth-century American whose credentials are "ambiguous,"

vii

will teach you how to tame it and ride it if you'll only stop horsing around and make some lists.

Since disorganized people tend to stick together like birds of a feather, you might not even *know* a well-organized person—or recognize one if you bumped into him/her. Actually, that was my situation, so my editor—who is on record as saying he would testify in court that I am the most disorganized author he had ever wet-nursed—naturally assigned me to do a book on getting organized.

"Can you do it?" he asked.

"Foolish question," I replied, blowing smoke. And I went home, feeling exactly as I had during World War II when, having demonstrated my abject fear of guns and my inability to strip down even an M-1 rifle, I was made gunnery officer of my destroyer escort. We won the war anyway, though the pilots of two American planes in the Pacific are still looking for me.

At home I put a lined yellow pad in front of me, along with a tall vodka tonic. I doodled on the one and sipped the other. In a moment, I was fast asleep, dreaming feverishly about writing a tour de force on getting organized. But how? What? It was like asking Howard Cosell to write a book on the glories of silence, or Yogi Berra on syntax, or Richard Nixon on morality. I dozed fitfully, certain that—as an author—I was about to sink without a trace, but was that so terrible? I had also risen without a trace. Maybe I could consult some expert who could shape me up and ship me out. Sure enough, in my anxious dream, the solution to my problem emerged. My sagacious editor, protecting Doubleday's flank against imminent disaster, arranged for me to have lunch with a FOP (Finely Organized Person) to prepare me for my prodigious research for this book.

She was already at the restaurant when I hurried in, my charisma aglow with sweat. Smiling, she beckoned me to take the stool next to her at the bar.

"Hi, there. I'm Alexis. I've ordered a martini for me and a bloody Mary for you. Our table will be ready in five minutes. Glad to meetcha."

"Me, too," I said. "But how did you know it was me? And how do you know I drink bloody Marys?"

"Preparation," she smiled, showing gleaming teeth and pink gums. "I have your picture, your bio and the publisher's file on your personal habits, including dietary, so I've ordered *moules* for you, I hope you don't find me pushy."

"No, no, no," I murmured. "Do you go to such pains whenever you meet someone? Or am I getting the VIP treatment?"

"Not at all," she said, signaling the head waiter with her left pinky that we were ready for our table. "I don't believe life should be a grab bag. I anticipate, I plan, I don't get hit from the blind side. Waiter, please, another round and have the drinks brought to our table."

As we reached our table, I had a momentary fear that she would help *me* to my seat, but no, she waited for me to do the honors for her. I pushed her chair a bit too heavily and toppled her into the chair. I felt gauche and irritated. Who needs to take a computer to lunch? And was my publisher picking up the tab? I forgot.

Dispatching the waiter to find a bottle of Lafite Rothschild 1963, she disarmed me with a soft, self-deprecating smile. "Don't be overwhelmed by my superb organization," she said. "I'm anal compulsive. Everything must be orderly. It's just my *shtik*. Please don't be put off by my controlled surface, there's probably a wild boar stalking inside of me."

"Oh, no bore you," I said, laughing uproariously at my little bon mot.

Lunch was elegant and the Rothschild was superb. As we dallied over coffee, Alexis whipped open her purse and produced a list which she placed on the table. "Our little agenda," she said.

"Agenda? You've got an agenda? Why?"

"Why not? It's now 1:37," she explained, "and I must be at my hairdresser at 2:30, so why should we just sit here and *phumphke*? Let's cover the items we're here to talk about. Time is life. Why waste it?"

Alexis took out a cigarette. "I permit myself three of these a day—one after each meal." She smiled.

I flipped my bic and Alexis said, "Thank you. First, do you have any questions? After all, you're the writer and you're supposed to be researching me. So be my guest."

"Yes," I said. "You seem to have your life so tightly planned, is there any room for spontaneity, for impulsiveness?"

"No," she replied. "Impulsiveness is for animals, children and neurotics. I always know what I'm doing, always in control, always calculating, if you will."

"My God," I exclaimed, "you're not *human*, Alexis. You're a *machine*, a computer, a female Rube Goldberg."

To my consternation, she burst into tears. Not softly either. She sobbed loudly, uncontrollably, her breath coming in short pants, her bosom heaving to leeward.

"Oh, forgive me," I pleaded, patting her shoulders as she wailed head down on the table. I felt miserable. She felt miserable. The head water hovered overhead, looking miserable. It was a scene from *Les Miserables*. I knew I should rescue the situation, but I felt immobilized, frozen.

Suddenly she threw back her head, wiped the tears from her eyes, sipped some coffee and smiled brilliantly. "See? I can be spontaneous if I want. But did you like it? My coming off the wall with that poor-me routine threw you for a loop. Being badly organized you didn't know what to do, did you?"

"No, not really."

"What you should have done is hand me your hankie. If I persisted in my hysterics, you should have slapped me. Then you should have paid the bill, called a cab and dropped me at my hairdresser, saying like Clark Gable in *Gone with the Wind*, 'Frankly, I don't give a damn.' You have to be prepared!"

"Ye gods, that whole thing was just an act?"

"Of course," she purred. "You have another question?"

"Tell me, Alexis, are you married, and how does *he* take you?"

"Yes I am, and he takes me in the standard missionary position. Any other questions?"

"No, I mean, sorry, I wasn't probing. I'll bet *you* keep the social calendar, make the decisions, buy his clothes, pick the car, make the lists, arrange the vacations, cover the plants with pantyhose, pay the bills, raise the kids, organize the weekends, the whole *shmeer,* right?"

"Right!" she replied.

"And doesn't that castrate him?"

"*Au contraire.* It relieves him of unnecessary distractions so he can be free to be fully a man, a complete husband, and devoted companion."

"Wow," I muttered. "What does your husband do for a living?"

"Oh, nothing. He keeps house. Passes the time making obscene phone calls. He's a dear, but he's not well enough organized to arrange anything more complicated than a two-car funeral."

"I see," I saw, not seeing anything and trying to figure out how to escape. "Then you're the breadwinner? But I don't get it. What do *you* do for a living?"

"Oh, didn't your editor tell you? I run FOP (Finely Organized People). I advise people, and I charge one hundred dollars an hour." She looked at her watch significantly.

"Oh, oh," I said nervously. "I see it coming."

"Shall I bill you or our publisher?" she asked brightly, springing to her feet.

"Are you kidding?" I asked, laughing.

"*Ciao,*" she said, handing me the bill* and disappearing into the street, as smooth and smartly organized as a pogrom.

---

* Doubleday, of course, refused to pay Alexis' bill, not to mention the restaurant tab, and neither of them would take my American Express Card. The whole thing was a total loss and exacerbated my hemorrhoids from bed to worse. Thank goodness it was only a dream, not to say nightmare!

YOU PACKED THE CAT
IN THE SUITCASE?!
You Gotta Get Organized

CHAPTER 1.

A Man's Home Is His Hassle

A man's home is his hassle. A house is not a home, sweet
home if it is as disordered and nerve-jangling as Grand Central Station. You don't have to be stuffy to wish some order in
the operation of the house. Look at your house, for example.
Must everything be an emergency? Must the telephone always
be one step away from being shut off by Ma Bell? Do you always have to be embroiled in a war of nerves with the newspaper delivery service? Do the television, the record player,
the radio and the children have to blare at the same time? Do
you have to rush to the railroad station, sloshing coffee and
blasting your auto horn just as the train doors are closing? Is
it necessary to discover that your plane departs from Dulles
only after you have battled traffic to National? Is there a law
that prevents you from getting a number of tokens in advance
so you don't have to have apoplexy on that long subway line?
You've lived long enough—and spun your wheels long enough
—to begin a new lifestyle. The time has come to organize your
life, plan ahead, budget your time, reduce the rush-hour at-
mosphere that has turned you into a whirling dervish. Stop
punching pillows. Bring a measure of serenity into your home
life.

How?

1

1. Get out of bed already

The root of your problem is that you don't arise early enough. You are backed up before you even start the day. Get an alarm clock that really splits the air and set it at least sixty minutes earlier than your usual awakening. As things stand (or sleep) now, by the time you drag yourself out of bed you have twenty-three minutes to shower, perform your ablutions, argue with your mate, dress, avoid calisthenics, eat, drink coffee, scan the front page and race to the station. Ridiculous and bad for the system.

Under the new regimen, you will have twenty minutes for jogging, fifteen minutes for meditating, four more minutes for breakfast and time for a leisurely stroll to the station, as well as time to board the train, feeling alive and tingling, to settle comfortably in a seat where you will fall asleep in total exhaustion. This has the additional advantage of sparing you conversation with your loquacious neighbor, Jacques, who is notorious in the neighborhood because he has the temerity *not* to bring a newspaper or a book on the train. If this all doesn't work, sleep till noon and the hell with Rule 1.

2. Everything has its place

Your present non-system is absurd. Did you ever figure out how much of your life is spent looking for things around the house? What sense does it make for your glasses (four pairs) to be scattered in such places as under the car seat, inside the oven, beneath the love seat and atop the *National Enquirer* rack at the local supermarket? Why do you have to go through such a *tsimmes* to find a pair of scissors? Or to locate a stamp (when you could swear you bought a book of them the day before)? Or to find the magazine section of the New York *Times* when rushing to the bathroom? Surely you need not waste so much energy on the minutiae of daily living. You can organize your home so that each item is at your fingertips on pegboards.

Here's how: (a) Move. Your present house or apartment is over the brink. There is no way to bring order out of that *abattoir*. It's either too small or too large. Sell it or bulldoze it and start from scratch.

(b) Now that you have moved, things can begin. You can throw away all the furniture and knickknacks that the movers damaged, which is a good start. Now set aside one wall in each room and paint it as a wall map, identifying every object in the room by its quadrant and sector. Divide the room across by color, from 1 to 10, nailing the identifying chart on the adjacent wall.

3. How to fix things around the house before the whole place falls in on you

You are not handy, let's grant that, but it doesn't take a mechanical genius to do minor repairs and to avert disasters. If the roof has a small leak, an ostrichlike procrastination will only bring on a situation in which the next hurricane will float your family out to the street. Similarly, you don't have to be a MIT engineer to fix the little doohickey causing the leak in the upstairs bathroom. Is it necessary to postpone the chore until your boss comes for dinner and, using your broken toilet, flushes with chagrin? Isn't the grass easier to mow if you do it weekly instead of weakly when it looks like elephant grass? What does it gain you to put off the inevitable trial of mounting the storm windows until Groundhog Day of every year? Grow up, for heaven's sake!

Why not try the poor-me technique? Take a ladder outside, lamely circle the job for an hour or so, limp a little (didn't you pull a muscle once playing tennis?), look confused and helpless, fall off the ladder from the second rung and curse your fate. By this time, one of your neighbors (or relatives) will be attracted by the scent of disaster and—if you play your cards right—will show you how to do it. By doing it! This is the Tom Sawyer technique. It usually works, but here too, you may have to move frequently as your neighbors get used up. *Otherwise hire a handyman and cut your losses.*

4. Planning your entertainment

Why should you always decide at the last minute to go to a play, a movie or a game? Why run the risk of getting there too late (you haven't seen the first act of an opera at the Met yet?) or not getting a ticket to the show or seeing a movie which is a clinker? A little advance preparation can resolve these difficulties.

For example, here's how to go to a movie. Make up a movie book. Cut out all the movie reviews and paste them into a notebook. Enter how much each movie house charges—underline the dollar theaters. Note the parking situation at each place and the travel directions from home. Leave room for comments from friends about each film and the various neighborhood theaters. Also make note on the refreshments available at each (no Nibs), as well as the behavior of the audience (talking right through the climax, raucous, rolling empty bottles, clapping when movie ends or jeering the reel-changing, hooting pictures of Carter, not removing hats, usher shushing kids, bums sleeping in the back row, stereo bursting your eardrums or smoking in the balcony only). *Better you should watch TV.*

5. *Watching television*
The average American child, connected to the TV set by the eyeballs, becomes catatonic before he is six years old. Many authorities think that such an overdose of sex and violence has deleterious effects on the kids—and explains in part why they grow up to be either muggers or muggees. Be that as it may, that is the least of *our* concern. Our concern is that with children always watching the TV, when do *we* get to watch?

The trick is—as always—to organize. Get started in your organizing as soon as you are married. Observe zero population because otherwise you'll need a color TV set for each child, and the typical American family has 2.6 black and white children.

6. *Organizing your budget*
This is a monthly headache for everyone, but the dicey way you mishandle it makes bills a daily migraine. Why must you be one step ahead (or behind) the warnings, dunnings and ultimata of the computers every month? Why do you have to live on a diet of anxiety, fear, guilt and fury, especially when a little planning can turn this ordeal into a minor administrative chore? Why can't you remember to put a star in the checkbook for each deductible payment?

You've got to put an end to the chaos in which you and your mate write checks separately and never tell each other. You should have realized that you had to change the *status quo* (which is defined as the mess you're in) when the bank called and said you were overdrawn and you hollered at your wife and she said, "How can that be, I still have six blank checks in my book?"

Perhaps what you need is zero-based budgeting.

There must be a better way to handle your banking than the chaos that marks it now. Your problems are legion. You forget to enter the amounts of your checks in your book. You lose your checkbook. They're always slapping penalties on you for overdrafts. When you tally at the end of the month (or the tenth of the next) you go by the latest bank statement, forgetting that it does not show the checks that have not yet cleared, thus giving you a fake illusion of solvency.

There is a way to solve this: Change banks every month. Why not? You're likely to get a gift for your new account, and the new bank will treat you with the same icy anonymity that always greeted you at the old place where you banked for ten years.

Look especially for banks with special features—free checking, long hours, Saturday openings, high interest, gifts, drive-in windows, chesty tellers. If possible, find a bank that makes you feel at home. Most banks have guards, tellers and vice-presidents who look you over with blank suspicion and make you feel like the Godfather.

But if, as seems likely, you cannot learn to cope with banks and with bills, there is one ultimate solution: Set up an account for household expenses and *pay your accountant* to PAY ALL YOUR BILLS! Let *his* mother worry!

7. Make lists

How will you be able to use your time properly if you are subject to whim and impulse? Think ahead. Make lists and keep them tucked in your wallet or purse so you won't lose them. Here is a model list:

Sharpen the pencils
Renew auto license

Don't forget Sophie's birthday, she's been hinting for weeks

Tell everyone must jiggle handle after flushing

Do we have mice? Put saccharine in the traps

RSVP Cousin Frank's wedding. Is this his fourth or fifth?

Write letter to the *Times* about the LIRR

What's this about a laser beam to knock out hemorrhoids?

Never, never start crossword puzzle again

Must organize the spices alphabetically

Label each pair of scissors by task (hair, paper, plants, chives, self-defense, toenails)

Why not different color socks for each member of the family?

Stop with the coffee already

Cigarettes also

Be romantic—wife's pissed

Pick up new tennis balls

Renew reading *Herzog* for seventh time; will I ever finish it?

Why do we have three different appointment calendars? Combine them.

8. *Keep your records*

Why not establish a memory bank? It could be a filing cabinet. Use it for appliance-maintenance pamphlets, receipts, warranties and credit card numbers (first throwing away all cards from before 1965). In the memory bank, also keep full records of all major repairs and improvements on the suburban house, so you won't get clobbered with a staggering capital gains tax when the kids grow up, who has to clean such a big house, and you're ready to sell the White Elephant and move into the renovated brownstone in the inner city (which, of course, turns out to be the tenement your grandparents fled two generations ago).

REASONS WHY YOU'RE SO DISORGANIZED

One of your troubles is that you NEVER THROW ANYTHING AWAY. Heaven knows why, but as you get older you are disappearing slowly under the accumulated debris of your life. It is one thing to save baby pictures and the charming memorabilia of yesteryear, but the medical bills of 1955 can have little sentimental attraction and they clutter your files. How many years must you worry about the IRS appearing for an audit?

In an acquisitive society, you will sink under the weight of *chozzerai* (Latin for *chotchke*) if you do not throw things away when they have outlived their usefulness. Do you realize you have three old inoperable toasters in the garage? For what possible purpose? And you still have all the children's ice skates, even though the children are now fully grown and you've been on thin ice for years. Why can't you throw the stuff away? What good now are the bubble gum cards, the bottle caps, the old copies of *P.M.* and the moldy baseball gloves of your childhood? Are you emulating the Collier brothers? The ship is sinking unless you jettison the excess baggage of your life—and the quicker the better.

If you can't just heave it all away, organize a Tag Sale or a Garage Sale. Sell your old garbage pails, electric cords, rusty file cabinets, your sway-back Ping-pong table, your 1948 moth-eaten badminton net, your 1956 set of Encyclopedia Americana (missing only volumes B, M, S and W), seven busted lamps, a perforated hose and a brand-new toilet seat (bright red, your spouse would never sit still when you tried to install it), towels from the Cairo Hilton. A little free enterprise will free up your house—and let your neighbors worry!

How to throw alway old obsolete friends has been organized under Chapter 4 (for reasons that escape us. Ed.).

The *status quo* has got to go. You simply cannot function this way anymore. Each evening when you get home, the first thing you do—after checking to see what has been burgled—is to get the mail. Standing at the mail box, you riffle through the stuff, see that it is mostly bills and political junk mail and you grunt unhappily and throw the whole pile either (a) on

7

top of the TV set, thinking you'll sort it out during the commercials; (b) into the magazine rack; (c) on the kitchen counter; (d) on the night table next to your bed; (e) next to the commode; or (f) in the basement, next to the pool table, on which your wife irons the laundry.

Who can live like that? Is it too much trouble to separate the mail into junk to be thrown away immediately (postcards from your mother's senile aunt may or may not fall into this category), bills to be paid, letters to be answered? You say to yourself that if the U. S. Government can't organize its mail system, how can you organize yours, right? Wrong!

Certainly your present "system" (which is made up of equal parts of lassitude, sloth and insouciance) is counterproductive. Its effects are ruinous and predictable. It results in a terrible running battle with the telephone company which cuts off your service while you insist (finally persuading *yourself* without in any way persuading *their computer*) that they never sent you the bill in the first place. It results in hours of searching in smelly garbage pails for missing wedding invitations. It leads to sibilant long-distance telephone calls from your mother in Miami demanding to know, in guilt-edged *mama-loshen,* "So why didn't you answer my last letter?" resulting in a lame, "What letter is *that?*" from your end of the line. It leads, in short, to wasting time, spinning wheels, running in place and making a damn fool of yourself.

Get with it. A neat and simple system would solve your problem. Here it is: Have a carpenter build you a mail disposal cabinet with well-organized bins, as below:

PERSONAL MAIL

Letters I'll answer one of these days

Letters I'll never get around to answering, but will feel guilty throwing away right away (wait 30 days)

Letters I'll stamp "return to sender" and/or "moved, address unknown"

Save the stamps

Bills I'll pay one of these days
Dunning bills
Bills I'll challenge and drive them crazy with
If I pay this, is it tax deductible?

2ND AND 3RD CLASS MAIL .

To be thrown away immediately, if not sooner
Meeting notices from church or synagogue of my faith
and political clubs and civic associations, so I can keep
track of the meetings I don't attend
Pornographic literature—hold for a slow day

If your mail is uninteresting and third class, it is probably
because you are too lazy to write your friends and relatives.
So it's not surprising they long since stopped writing you.
Here's the trick. After dinner, when the family is just lolly-
gagging around, bring out the tape recorder and *talk* a letter
to a friend. It will be faster if you all talk at once—but less orderly. But, please, don't forget to mail the tape immediately.
In all that confusion, a welter of unmarked tapes sitting
around for months could well be the last straw.

There are two types of people: those who *write* books and
those who *read* them. If you are one of the former, fine. If the
latter, let's face the truth that you are drowning in books—
new and old—and you haven't finished reading a book in
seven lean years. In fact, you have now fallen asleep on Alex
Haley's *Roots* twenty-seven times and you have developed the
dreadful habit at social gatherings of making comments about
new books of which the total extent of your familiarity is a
once-over-lightly review in the New York *Times*. For shame!

So how can you organize your time and energy for reading?
Firstly, cancel the *Times*. You've been hooked long enough
and forswearing the *Times* will free up six and a half hours
each week for reading something more enduring than the
daily paper.

9

Secondly, you must learn to read without nodding off. Reading in bed or stretched out on a recliner or bouncing on a commuter train or flat on your back on a chaise lounge—all these positions are bad news. Sominex should only knock you out as quickly. One year you did not get past page 97 of *Portnoy's Complaint* for an entire summer. (If it seemed to you Alex was playing with himself every time you picked up the book, he was.) You must learn to read under tension, perhaps perched on the top of a ladder or grabbing a strap on a lurching subway or while sitting in a bathtub. If you fail to keep your eyes open and reading, you will have to pay the consequences, which is a lot better than carrying a book around unread until you start to get summonses from the library.

There's another useful tip: Take a course in speed reading. What with your instant sleepiness and your snail's pace reading speed when awake, it is foolish for you to take all those detours, such as: "What does 'tumescent' mean? How do you spell it? How would you use it in a sentence? What does he mean here? And where the hell is the dictionary, so a person can look up a new word?" Learn to get at the pith. Woody Allen took speed reading and, when asked what *War and Peace* was about, answered, "Russia." You, too, should learn to burrow through a book, extract the essence, savor it fondly and enjoy a sense of fulfillment and completion. *Liber interruptus* has afflicted you most of your life, and it's time for a change.

If you fail to master all the above, it is time to buy a second home in the country. The beauty part about this is that you can then have a plaque on both your houses. Also, while your gardener is mowing *your* lawn, you can drive five hours to your house in the country in order to mow the *other* lawn, provided you learn to breathe the clean air without choking.

And how can anyone expect you to keep track of your bills and mail when you are always at the wrong home? In addition, the country home is a great "out" to avoid bothersome obligations. When they call you for a church bazaar or a party for the office nudnik, or to meet with an IRS agent, you can always say; "Sorry, we'll be at our country place."

The secret of a successful country house is simple: no telephone! If your teen-age children demand a telephone, *batter* them because battered children are common in the country and in the city, and they are certainly preferable to the parade of relatives and friends who, in three months, would reduce you and your mate to weary innkeepers dreaming of escape back to the first house. Absence of a telephone is sure to clear your sinuses.

AND NOW TEST YOURSELF

1. When you're not wearing your glasses, you keep them:

   A. on top of your head
   B. swinging from your Phi Beta Kappa chain
   C. in a case where they belong
   D. stuffed into the book you're reading
   E. for New Eyes for the Needy

2. You return library books:

   A. before they expire
   B. before *you* expire
   C. under subpoena
   D. under protest
   E. under the table, your sister is the librarian

3. When it comes to special occasions like birthdays and anniversaries, you:

   A. always remember
   B. are out of town
   C. have to be reminded
   D. remember the next day
   E. speak softly and make a big scene

CHAPTER 2.

You Think You Are Thoreau

In some ways, you are very courageous. You use the subways and the bus. You walk the streets of New York at night without a battle helmet. When a stranger asks you for directions, you do not run away on the ground that it is better to be safe than sorry. You carry no guns and, indeed, you still sign petitions for gun control. You continue to smoke even though your doctor says your lungs look like used charcoal and your dentist says your mouth is "an open furnace." You gorge yourself with saccharine, even though—placed in mousetraps in the garage—it has decimated your rat population. Your physical courage is not exactly formidable—nobody ever calls you "ballsy," no—but you are not craven or chicken either.

No, your Achilles heel is the paper form you have to fill out. Whether it is your income tax, your automobile registration, your passport, your Blue Cross medical, your auto accident form or any other such bureaucratic intrusion, you are reduced to sweaty helplessness. If it is a form without a deadline, you'll stuff it behind the antique clock. If it has to be notarized and/or it has some legal threat about false information, you'll certainly lose it. If your mate or some *apparatchik* finally puts the heat on you to fill out the cursed thing, you will screw it up beyond description and then mail it—misaddressed and unstamped—to Coty, Wyoming.

Why this hang-up? You have—of course—draped your nakedness with false armor. To you, this contempt for forms is your assertion of your humanity against the computerized, Big Brother welfare state. You think you are Thoreau, walking on the water at Walden, defying the heavy hand of Authority. Fat chance! You are not striking a blow for individual autonomy, the sacred right to be left alone. You are probably acting out a childish fear, which may date back to the seat-wetting panic you experienced in the third grade when you faced your first arithmetic test. Now, as an adult, you still turn into a pillar of salt when your eye glazes on a blank form demanding to be completed. You can't hack it, so you pass the buck. Who can live that way?

And when you do—finally—complete the form, it looks like the jottings of a Mongolian idiot. Here is one form you filled out for your car registration:

NAME: *Harold Ferguson*

ADDRESS: *We're thinking of moving; I'll get back to you.*

SEX: *Average twice a week, more in the winter.*

COLOR OF EYES: *Mauve.*

HEIGHT: *I always spelled it "heighth" with an "h"; am I off base?*

MAKE OF CAR: *Toyota, good mileage, don't hike my tax, please.*

COLOR: *I'm white, but I have 4 black friends and practice affirmative action and ordinary courtesy.*

WEIGHT: *Do you mean the car, myself, or myself in the car.*

PREVIOUS ACCIDENTS: *Fell down the cellar steps and split my tongue; threw out my back playing touch football*

13

with the kids; twisted my ankle escaping from what I thought was mugger—turned out Hare Krishna giving me a flower.

INSURANCE: *My wife would get $120,000 if I died just like that, but $240,000 if on a plane or in a car, and my wife jokes that I should please rush into the car if I feel a stroke coming on, ha ha.*

So hire a smart high school kid for $2.00 an hour and let *his* mother worry!

CHAPTER 3.

Losing Through Intimidation at the Office

Why is your office constantly aflutter? Where is it written that every hour must erupt in a fresh crisis? Careful advance planning and intelligent organization of your time can put even your act together. Here are some guidelines which, if applied, can lower your frenzy and up your efficiency, as you progress through the day.

1. Commuter train
Your day at the office begins on the commuter train—badly. Actually, commuting doesn't have to be the harrowing hassle you've made of it. It could be a relaxing, restful interlude. Why do you have to roar into the station with seven seconds time to buy a ticket and a newspaper and down the rest of your coffee? It's folly and murder on your constitution. There are ways to transform this ordeal into easy-going serenity.

a. Learn how to fold your newspaper already. Seated in the middle of a three-seater, there is no way you can turn the pages of the New York *Times* in the normal manner. You must fold it in half vertically and then read one section at a time. Perhaps once you get this technique down, you will avoid the ugly incidents of recent years in which your neighbor, incensed by your newspaper in his face, pulled your hat down over your ears.

You can, of course, go bareheaded . . . or switch to the tabloid paper, but in your suburb that is *déclassé*. So take a later train that is uncrowded and spread your *Times* all over the car.

b. To enjoy your newspaper and/or a little snooze, avoid everyone you know on the train. Wear dark glasses, false nose and fake sideburns. Keep your eyes down, as if you have dropped your ticket or are looking for lost coins on the floor, so your eyes don't meet those of a wordy neighbor, relative or a hyper member of the local civic association who is a walking spiel in search of an audience. Find a double seat occupied by a small stranger (preferably mute), drop into the unoccupied seat and brandish the paper so that you are screened off from any potential conversationalists. If the small stranger next to you tries to strike up a conversation, holler rape and wake up the conductor to have the offender put off at Jamaica.

c. Do not lose your brief case because they have not yet found your last one, which—because of its bizarre contents—you were too embarrassed to inquire after.

2. *Your desk*

Your office is a shambles as anyone can see by looking at the top of your desk. Why does it have all that debris heaped and piled on it? Do you really need seven ash trays (stolen from hotels in European cities), your appointment calendars dating back to 1964 (in case the IRS belatedly comes after you), pictures of your ex-wife and ex-children, a busted pair of scissors, a nail clip, a map of the New York City subway system, a plaque saying, "Our streets are not safe, our parks are not safe, our homes are not safe, but we have 24-hour safety in our armpits—you call that priorities?" and an Italian-English dictionary (which, considering that the only Italian words you know are *pizza* and *andiamo,* is ridiculous). Your problem at the office replicates your problem at home: *You have never learned to throw anything away.*

The litter on your desk only highlights those mountains of

mail . . . one for first class; one for second, third and fourth class; one for internal memoranda. Considering how long you have shuffled those papers from one pile to another, would it really cause any harm if you dumped it all into the waste-basket and started fresh? Cut your losses, including that 1973 letter offering to put you in "Who's Who on the West Side of St. Paul, Minnesota," if you promise to buy the book when it is published.

There are three ways to clear your desk. One is to answer your mail; the second is to distribute it in your drawers; and the third is to file it daily in the proverbial circular file and see whose ox is gored, if anyone's. Since you are not the type (Libra is) to answer the stuff, and you lack the gumption to toss it away, stuff it into your desk drawers. Do it system-atically, not at random, Mark one drawer MAIL FROM PESTS AND NUDNIKS; another TICKLER FILE, consisting of good jokes sent in from the salesmen in the field; another F. U. File, meaning follow-up, but not until they show they care enough to write again, and then you can say, "Hey, you didn't respond to my first letter." Only 3 per cent of your cor-respondents are sufficiently motivated—and organized—to do that, so why push yourself?

Another drawer should be reserved for LEISURE-TIME READING—any letter or document that is longer than four pages single-spaced.

A friend of mine operates a busy office in Tulsa but, having a modern Swedish desk with a small surface and no drawers, files his papers under the rug. He has been squirreling papers under the rug like that for ten years and walking into his sway-backed office is like entering the funny room at the car-nival. You can get seasick walking on his rug, but you have to be impressed with his sure grasp of where every document is lodged. When he needs a document, he bellyflops under the rug headfirst, squirms to the precise spot as gracefully as an olive dropping through the stomach of a skinny girl in a leo-tard, and emerges with the paper in his beak. It isn't fancy, but it works and it makes you wonder what's wrong with sweeping things under the rug.

But don't go overboard. An absolutely whistle-clean desk is

worse than a littered desk. An empty desk bespeaks an empty soul and a tight ass. Why have a desk at all if you keep nothing on top of it? After all, a desk is a barrier to communicating with another person. The desk between puts you in authority—and your visitor down. Don't make the mistake of getting out from behind it and pulling up a chair alongside your visitor, thus making you true equals. Keep your distance and your dignity, or what's an office for?

3. *Get rid of the mail each day*

This may seem a chicken goal, but don't underestimate it. If your desk looks like war-torn Belfast, the jumble has got to affect you. If you have to thrash through mountains of flotsam and jetsam to find an interoffice memo, you are behind the eight-ball before you even begin your day. Instead of tossing the mail into the maw of your desk, dispose of each day's mail before the sun sets. You have these options:

A. The circular file
B. Buck it to one of your associates
C. Place it in the tickler file for future attention. This has the virtue of getting it off your desk and onto your secretary's.
D. Tell your secretary to answer it: "Give him a variation of Form 16C" (which says, in essence, "Yours is an interesting idea, but unfortunately budgetary strictures, etc., etc.")
E. Send along an executive buck-passer memo as follows:
    ( ) IF HE PHONES, I'M OUT
    ( ) MAKE 5 CARBONS, CIRCULATE, THEN FILE
    ( ) TOO EXPENSIVE
    ( ) TOO CHINTZY
    ( ) YOU KNOW WHERE YOU CAN PUT THIS
    ( ) HAS THE BOSS SEEN THIS YET? (If he likes it, so do I)
    ( ) WHO ELSE KNOWS ABOUT THIS?
    ( ) WHERE ARE YOU COMING FROM?
    ( ) YOU MUST BE KIDDING!

( ) ARE YOU AFTER MY JOB?
( ) DON'T CALL ME . . . I'LL CALL YOU ON THE
WATTS LINE
( ) RETURN TO SENDER
( ) UP YOURS
( ) MIND IF I FRAME THIS?
( ) YES   ( ) NO   ( ) MAYBE
( ) QUIT WHILE YOU'RE WINNING
( ) WHOSE SIDE ARE YOU ON?!
( ) THIS SHMUCK SHOULD BE HOISTED AND SHACKLED
( ) FILL ME IN
( ) DON'T FILL ME IN
( ) WHO DREAMED UP THIS ABORTION?
MUST HAVE   ( ) Tomorrow   ( ) Right
away   ( ) Next month   ( ) A meet-
ing on this
( ) LET ——— DO IT
( ) HIRE THIS WOMAN
( ) FIRE THIS WOMAN
( ) OH, OH, THE ANIMALS ARE RATTLING THE CAGE!
( ) HOW LONG HAS THIS BEEN GOING ON?
( ) IS IT TAX DEDUCTIBLE?
( ) WHAT PUTZ PUT THIS IN WRITING?
( ) THE MORE YOU EXPLAIN IT, THE MORE I DON'T
UNDERSTAND IT
( ) TAKE A COLD SHOWER
( ) CONFIDENTIAL . . . Let's not let anyone know
we're that stupid
( ) BURN BEFORE READING

4. Let your secretary know who's boss
This is vital, but only if the answer is *you*. If your secretary
has already arrogated your authority—or thinks he/she has,
which may be the same thing—better plan to get rid of either
her or you. If this calamity hasn't happened yet, don't make
the common chic mistake in this age of telling her you are co-
equals, associates, partners in a common cause. That is both
false and cruel. It's your neck that is on the block in your
outfit, and her job is to help you and to protect your tail . . .

if not your neck. If her women's lib expectations are too exalted to accept so humble a role—if she gags on the title "secretary" and is touting herself as "associate"—get rid of her immediately, if not sooner.

Also, don't slide into a buddy-buddy relationship with your secretary. Except for a hanky-panky relationship, nothing could be worse for the organization of the office. Each of you must know and accept his/her place. Hers is banging away at the typewriter. Yours is batting the breeze with other executives. If that is a lousy authoritarian deal, go fight City Hall. She does not *have* to get coffee for you, of course—she's a free agent—but you don't *have* to certify her trumped-up time sheets either.

5. *Cut down on small talk*

There is the famous apocryphal story of Pope John showing a delegation through the Vatican. One of the visitors, obviously impressed, asked the pontiff how many people work at the Vatican. The Holy Father thought a moment and said, "About half." That's about par for most offices.

One reason for the low productivity in many offices is the phenomenon of *shmoosing*. *Shmoosing* is a leisurely form of small talk or idle chatter. If a secret tape recorder were on in your office, what would it catch on a given day? Probably an hour of the latest office jokes, an hour of anecdotes (some of your fellow executives are in their anecdotage), an hour of personal problems ("My wife says, 'Look, Max, I can check my breasts *myself.'* ") and an hour of office gossip ("Hal Herlicky is organizing a *coup d'état* against you; you're Number One on his Enemy List."); the balance of the time is wasted on meetings.

This type allocation of time is an abuse of the company and it is unconscionable. Something must be done to reorder priorities in your office and cut down on *shmoosing*. Here's the ticket:

6. *Never leave your door open*

It's an open invitation for the *shmoozers* to invade. Keep your door closed and locked. If someone wants to see you, make him/her get an appointment from your secretary and the appointment must *never* be open-ended—"You can have seven minutes at 2 P.M. Wednesday"—and must look like an awful intrusion into your tight schedule. To cut down on resultant paranoia against the power of your secretary ("That bitch hates my guts and keeps me away from you like she's a female cross between Ehrlichman and Haldeman. Why does she hate me? And who's running this office anyway, *you* or that power-mad *dame?*"), you might install a machine à la the local bakery, in which each applicant takes a number and then awaits a call from your secretary . . . first come, first served. They'll all resent you a bunch, of course, but they'll suspect you are a busy, high-powered executive and (behind the locked door) you can read the daily paper in peace, as well as enjoy your afternoon nap without getting swallowed up in Wheeler's wife's hysterectomy.

7. *Level of paranoia*
Every office maintains a certain level of paranoia which can be raised and lowered like a thermostat. Example:

BIG ENCHILADA: Hello there, son, how are you feeling?

WATSON: Good, sir.

BIG ENCHILADA: Really?

WATSON: (to himself) Oh, oh, why *shouldn't* I feel good? (to colleague standing nearby) What did the boss mean by *that?*

BIG ENCHILADA: (to himself) This character's cheerfulness depresses me. I don't trust him. (to the same colleague standing nearby) What's that smily fellow's name again?

8. *Keep a log*
You *think* you know how to spend your time each day, but you really don't. When you get home at night and your spouse wants to know what happened at the office, it isn't that you are "uncommunicative" (as your spouse thinks). It is that you can't really think of *anything* that happened that day. So keep

a log for one week—every conversation, every telephone call, every meeting. You will find that your week consisted mostly of interruptions. By whom? What for? Did one or two *nudniks* monopolize your time? Punch them out.

The secret of success—at the office and at home—is learning to say *"no."* "No" can be a beautiful word. The inability to say it causes more conflict and frustration than any other failure. Indecisiveness drains time and energy. Phony compromises paper over a problem and only delay decisions. You needn't feel guilty, nor do you have to be cruel and unfair, to say, "No, I do not have time." "No, I do not agree with you." "No, I do not approve your recommendation." "No" takes strength of character, but it is the shortest path between two points. Practice saying "no" for thirty minutes each day, and it will save you more time and liberate more of your productive resources and energies than drinking honey and popping vitamins.

The people under you, on the other hand, should be trained to say *"yes!"*

9. Dining in (at the office)
You and your office colleagues have been *derrière-garde* long enough. Your business lunches are too expensive, too time-consuming and too fattening. The time has come to organize yourself for in-house lunches. Just *shlep* a brown-paper bag from home, containing cheese, fruit, yogurt, or deveined shrimp, plus thinly sliced vegetables. After a delightful and modest lunch, you will feel grand (neither bloated nor broke) and you will also, of course, be a patsy for a "Big Mac Attack" an hour later which will propel you to McDonald's, three blocks away—that is, if you can fly there without stopping to devour two hot dogs and a falafel at curb-side temptations down the way.

The above brown-bag lunch is okay, and it will require of you a certain minimum of organization (the first week you'll leave the bag in the bus, until you learn to put a mailing address on it). Ideally, you could stuff your lunch into your brief case which—let's face it—you now use for pornographic magazines, nutty jokes Xeroxed at the office, and *TV Guide*. Whoever said life is *not* a free lunch?

But either go the brown-bag route or go out to a restaurant and take the martini route. Do *not* order up sandwiches to the office for your small business meeting. The order will not arrive until after 2:00 P.M. They will forget one sandwich and the lean corned beef will come glued to mayonnaise, and the pickles will drip brine on your desk, and you'll have to use Kleenex for napkins, and they'll give you ketchup instead of mustard, and plastic forks for the liquidy cole slaw, and the toasted white bread will be burned rye, and at least two colleagues you were hoping to avoid will join the debacle even before you can take an Alka Seltzer!

10. Hard work

Are you a workaholic? Do you work too hard? Put in exorbitant hours and still never get finished? The answer is not to work harder, but to organize yourself so that you can work less or not at all. The three-fold secret is to *decide,* to *delegate* and to *deliberate*. No longer can you live in accordance with the gospel of Tish Tosh that you are right and you are right and everything is quite correct.

Decisiveness is central because your chronic failure to make decisions is what saps your time and energy and louses up relationships across the board. Don't make a decision before you need to, but when the moment arrives, bite the bullet before it whizzes by you. You may make the wrong decision, but even that is probably less hurtful than worrying the decision —and yourself—to death.

In making a decision, bear in mind the three-fold application of Murphy's law:

a. Nothing is as easy as it looks;
b. Everything takes longer than it should;
c. Anything that you can wrong *will* go wrong.

Delegation of authority will save your life. If you can learn to delegate enough tasks you may not have to work at all, except for thirty minutes of heavy thinking each week (Put an "I'M THINKING" sign on your outer door). In those thirty minutes you may create the program, close the deal or conceive the strategy that justifies your salary for the week. (Or, of course, you may just have a nice erotic fantasy.) Why kill yourself with overwork if you can kill your associates?

Deliberation is also necessary. Why wait for the deadline? Why back and fill? Planning your work with deliberation will cut down on wasted motion. Why not double check the precise dimensions of the broken window before buying the glass? And, in working, don't gun your engine in fitful spurts. Work at a nice, even, cruising speed. It's less exhausting and more efficient and burns less gas on the stomach, thus alleviating your energy crisis.

11. Arriving and departing

There is an art to knowing when to arrive at the office and when to depart. If you get to work too early, it means your anxiety is showing. If you get there too late, you're hostile. If you arrive right on time, you're compulsive. If, on the other hand, you call in sick and go to sun at the beach, you're brimming over with mental health.

Departing must similarly be organized. If you are an executive, it is *déclassé* to leave on time, joining the mad rush of the hoi polloi on the elevator at three minutes to five. Instead, you should pack your brief case and leave either at three (after a martini lunch) or at 6:30 (for a business dinner meeting with martinis), being sure to tuck your cigarette into your brief case before entering the "No Smoking" elevator.

12. Make a list

Before leaving the office to go home, you should organize your brief case for night work at home, and—of course—make a list of what must be done on the morrow. Here is a sample list by a model executive:

Get an advance on salary—we're broke (again)
Go to the bank

Don't forget—Val owes me $10

Set up farewell party for Hank—he's been axed

Call your shrink—he's depressed, says you never call just to ask how *he* feels

Write memo to file on Hank—cover your ass

Invite Parness for lunch—his turn for the tab

Get tickets for game

Talk to boss—need a private john for class

AND NOW TEST YOURSELF

1. If you have lent twenty bucks to an office colleague:

    A. make a note and put it in your drawer

    B. ditto *his* drawer

    C. put in your tickler file (because he'll laugh in disbelief when you come to collect)

    D. write it off for IRS as uncollectible

    E. you'll get what you deserve (zilch)

2. If you are a commuter, you should buy a monthly commutation because it is cheaper, but

    A. you don't because you think: What if I get sick next week?

    B. you can't stand the long lines, so instead you get in line each *day* for a daily, costly ticket

    C. you think: What if I drop dead tomorrow?

    D. you always feel the railroad is so sleazy that such a large expenditure is a rip-off

    E. you and your mate have been talking about *moving* for twenty years, and wouldn't a monthly commutation ticket mortgage your future?

3. Because you like to clip and file interesting items from the daily paper, you

A. carry a handy little scissors (which doubles as antimugger defense)
B. mark the items for your secretary to clip (and then forget the paper on the subway)
C. never get past page six of the first section
D. drive your spouse up the wall by bringing home a perforated paper that looks more like confetti than the *Times*

CHAPTER 4.

If Your Host Is Polish,
Don't Tell Polish Jokes

If you are invited to someone's home and you have never been there before, you are entitled to certain information to help you decide whether or not to go. Just mail the following questionnaire to whomever RSVP'd you (it can be filled out in five minutes):

1. Do you have small children? List their ages.
2. Do the babies cry when strange people are in the house? Do you?
3. Do the children entertain—piano, magic, poetry, stampbooks, whatever?
4. How many guests? I mean, a party or a convention?
5. Do you have: A pool table? A Ping-pong table? A sauna? A jacuzzi? Orgies? A television set? A stereo?
6. Will you have a hired bartender dressed in Beafeater costume?
7. This isn't a surprise party, is it? If so, will there be public gift opening?
8. Will there be a maid bringing around hot and cold hors d'oeuvres?

9. Are you on the jet route to the airport?
10. Does the LIRR go through your kitchen?
11. Do you insist that your guests play games . . . charades, etc.?
12. Do you show home movies?
13. Porno?
14. Do you call each other "Mommy" and "Daddy"?
15. Will it take more than an hour to get to your place?
16. Will there be a gay bar?
17. Do you have a dog? A cat?
18. Do you tell Polish jokes?
19. Will we play cards?
20. Will you *call* cards?

Analyze the answers and decide for yourself!

The first thing about going out for a social evening is not to go unless you really *want* to. Also, don't go if the answer to #15 is "You can't miss it." If the evening promises to be a bummer (or there is a honey of a game on TV), here are some effective cop-outs:

1. Call and say you've come down with a bad case of scotch.
2. Have your secretary call and say you had to go suddenly to Rome for a private audience with the Pope (good *yontif*, Pontiff).
3. Call and say you racked up the Moped en route to the party and the cops are giving you a saliva test.
4. Send a telegram that you had a loss in the family—your Aunt Flo ran away to Acapulco to become a beachbum.
5. Get yourself arrested for flashing.

On the other hand, if you *do* go, organize yourselves in advance. Make sure your clothes are out of the cleaners in time. Buy a gift for the hostess *in advance* so you avoid the last-minute hassle with your mate, who insists on stopping and shopping on the way while you moan, groan and *kvetch*. Put gas in the car and check out the car *before* you leave. Bring a mimeographed "thank you" letter to mail to the host *on the way home*.

Also, prepare yourself for a sparkling evening. Tie one pair of glasses around your neck while gluing three other sets to the panel of your car. Have two or three good jokes (not Polish jokes; they're bigoted and, besides, your host is Polish) at the ready. Also, polish (pardon the pun) up a fresh anecdote or two and have three or four serviceable clichés on call. Be sure you have read an interesting book (or at least a review), seen a movie worth discussing and hold in reserve some penetrating insights into Jimmy Carter and Norman Lear.

Before entering the house, put "Hello, I am ———" tags on your coats and watch carefully where the host's son hurls your coats and hats. This will save you fifteen minutes of prime time later when everyone riots over piles of garments thrown on the beds, the maid and the bathtub. This will also avoid the irritating coat switches which leave you with a look-alike, ring-around-the collar London Fog with sleeves four inches longer than your own and with grubby and dog-eared gloves stuffed in the pockets where you're supposed to find your pipes, a tobacco pouch, an old timetable and a Con Ed bill.

Don't come to a party empty-handed; it's gauche. What to bring? Bring a *quid pro quo*. The *quid* is one of the gifts that people previously brought *you* when you entertained; the *quo* is bringing one of these same items to your present host, making sure that they are not the same people from whom you received them. This requires a little research; otherwise you will have egg on your face when the hostess pulls out your obscure Nigerian game and exclaims, "What the hell is *this?*" If you think *quid pro quo* is unworthy, you can always bring booze, flowers, wine or a book.

Speaking of which, this very volume would make a dandy gift, pleasing to the author if not to the host.

If you are not quite content with your gift, don't hand it to the host or hostess. Merely smuggle it onto the table among the other *quids* and head for the bar.

29

If it turns out to be one of those precious parties where they open the gifts publicly while everyone sits around and clucks, go over the wall (see "Escapes") or out the window. You won't be noticed unless, of course, it is a penthouse apartment.

Now, greeting the guests, you get caught up in the magnetic field drawing you to the bar. Organize yourself for a long evening. Don't go bonkers. One or two drinks, well nursed, should be adequate unless the party is a bomb, in which case fill up the tank. Don't make the mistake of pasting a dopey smile on your face and keeping it there the whole night. Remember, this is an age of angst. Fascinating people bear faces creased with weary anxiety, reflecting the weight of the human predicament or, more likely, gas on the stomach.

Glass in hand, reconnoiter the room, monitoring the various conversations before deciding which one to join. Stay away from the conversations focusing on science, Johnny Carson, the local country club, gardening, golf, the track, the stock market, insurance and the children and grandchildren. Zero in on baseball, sex, movies, politics, religion, or Ralph Nader, making sure you have a striking opening line to establish your presence. For example:

"Pardon me for breaking in like this, but it has been my growing impression that Jimmy Carter has transmogrified his Christian fundamentalism into an evangelical zeal for human rights throughout the world, utilizing the presidency as a bully pulpit, converting his well-advertised lust in the heart into a finely orchestrated passion for human rights, albeit selectively supplied," you say for openers.

A heavy silence afflicts the circle. "That's interesting, Harvey, but we were talking about the sex scandal at the country club."

"I know, I know," you press on. "But don't you realize that Carter's merely sublimating his own sexual conflicts into a puritanical foreign policy that screws the Russians but not the Iranians or the South Koreans?"

Their eyes glaze over, there is a shuffling of feet and a reshuffling of the cast of characters, and suddenly you are alone with the village bore (who, of course, thinks *you* are the village bore, silly creature that he is), conversing with the plants.

"How are you, Max?" you ask, knowing you have fallen into his trap.

"Terrible," he replies, and spells out in excruciating detail his automobile accident, his impotence, his wife's infidelities, his mother's infirmity, his business partner's instinct for embezzlement, the fact that his house is gradually collapsing under the shock of sonic booms of jets landing at Kennedy and his confident prediction that the human race will fornicate itself to an overpopulated extinction by year 2000.

"Terrific," you say, edging away. "Nobody's perfect, pal."

Spinning lightly to your left, you bump into your own wife. "Hi, honey, having fun?" You smile.

"Look, dear, I can talk to *you* anytime. We can't go on seeing each other like this. Why don't you mix?"

"I mix, I mix," you say. "Would you be interested in taking a little walk? A little arm-wrestling? Another drink? Whatever?"

"Darling," she replies, "it isn't nice to come to a party and talk to each other. Gross. At home you've got nothing to say to me. You stare at the boob tube and you don't know I'm alive. We finally get out with real people, and all of a sudden you discover my charm. Go mix!"

"I don't want to mix. I want to talk to you. I have conjugal rights," you whine.

"You're holding onto my choker. Bug off."

Conversation isn't everything at a party. There is also dining, but you must be on your toes here as well. Some hosts and hostesses have flaky ideas about fun.

Recently, in a party on Long Island, the wild rice was laced with LSD and ten couples freaked out of sight and drove home so spaced out that one couple parked necking *en flagrante* in the middle of the Holland Tunnel and they were photographed by four Mafia pornographers from Times Square. So use caution. Insist that the host taste everything first. Keep a geiger counter in your pocket and check out any morsel that looks doubtful. Don't be embarrassed. The stomach you save may be your own.

Escapes

If you wish to leave early, have a good excuse at the ready. Very serviceable are the following: "We have to rush home, I'm having a stroke in the morning." "Oy, I left the motor running . . ." "We just remembered—we have to make a *shivah* (condolence) call." "He forgot the battery for his pacemaker." But once you use your excuse, take off on the run. Lingering over farewells is one of the large defects of modern society. It has been noted that Germans and Englishmen leave without saying good-by, and Jews and Italians say good-by without leaving.

Short of pulling a Houdini, there is only one infallible way. At 11:15 you look at your watch and announce with appealing rue: "Oh, oh, we promised to get the baby-sitter home by midnight." There are four problems with this "out."

Firstly, be sure you have not come to the party with another couple. Making a quick escape is impossible if another couple—with their own rhythms and patterns—has to be coordinated with your sudden retreat. I mean, Lindbergh could never have flown the Atlantic with a committee.

Secondly, your car should not be trapped among other vehicles in the circular driveway but safely down the street—facing homeward and ready for a quick take-off. (Given the energy shortage, it's no longer good form to keep the motor idling.)

Thirdly, your mate had better be clued in. Otherwise, he/she may brush you off and continue the banal conversation into the wee hours or—even worse—he/she may stare at you like you've lost your marbles and exclaim: "What are you *talking* about? At four dollars an hour, the BABY-SITTER DOESN'T CARE IF WE GET HOME A WEEK FROM MONDAY!" Worst of all, he/she may say, "Darling, come off it, the *kids* are now twenty-four, twenty-one, nineteen and seventeen and we haven't had a baby-sitter for seven years. Are you getting senile?"

This, of course, leaves you with one foot out of the door and egg on your face—plus a San Andreas fault in your marital relations which will take more than Elmer's Glue to fix!

Going home—the review

After the excitement of such a pleasant evening with rich talk, little food and exciting company, going home is a pleasant chance to decompress, provided you and your mate are content to gossip and jointly savage everyone else at the party. It is time to write the *review*. "What kind of wine was that? It tasted like Listerine." "How did you like her Arab caftan? She looked like Yasir Arafat on a bad day." "Didn't you like their house? It's Holiday Inn Gothic." "I knew they were rich as soon as we sat down to dinner—*not much food!*"

But . . . don't let the drive home turn into a mutual review of our *own* performances, as follows:

WIFE: Well, Buster, you did it again.

HUSBAND: Did what again?

WIFE: Made a horse's ass of yourself, that's what.

HUSBAND: I was just enjoying myself. What's your beef this time?

WIFE: Did you have to stand up on the piano and do a gavotte?

HUSBAND: Oh, come off it. I don't even know what a gavotte is. You've done too many crossword puzzles. How many letters in "gavotte?"

WIFE: And how could you tell that black guy that stupid joke about the KKK guy who watches *Roots* backward so it'll have a happy ending?

HUSBAND: Oh, look I did that to give him a break. He's got to be tired of being the token black at these parties. Everybody was laying it on him, talking civil rights, *Roots* and black power. All those chic Volvo liberals leaking guilt and saying, "Right on, man." I liberated the poor guy with a joke. It was affirmative action!

WIFE: Yeah, you're a veritable Martin Luther King. And what about your hanky-panky on the balcony with that *zaftig* Lila? Were you liberating *her*, too?

HUSBAND: Oh, stop it. All you do is criticize. Did I criticize you for sitting there with that nutty crossword puzzle half the evening? Or for talking with food in your mouth?

WIFE: What food? There wasn't enough food there to fill my mouth. It's clear I can't take you anywhere.

HUSBAND: *Kvetch, kvetch!* I'm sick of your complaining. You drive my crazy. Some day I'm gonna—

WIFE: Be careful, you're tailgating!

HUSBAND: Give you such a shot in the *pisk*—

WIFE: You did it, buster, right up his tailgate!

AND NOW TEST YOURSELF

1. You do your Christmas shopping:

   A. the night before
   B. in midsummer
   C. with a little list
   D. with a lot of choler
   E. what Christmas shopping? You're Jewish!

2. You can always tell a superior restaurant by:

   A. candles on the tables
   B. ice cubes in the urinal
   C. if you ask the headwaiter whether the prices are moderate, he says, "If you have to ask, this is not the bistro for you."
   D. the tables are crowded against each other so that you can listen to everyone's conversation and virtually taste your neighbor's coq au vin

3. You arrive at a party:

   A. fashionably late
   B. already planning your exit

34

C. the wrong night
D. looking like a *shlepper* while everyone else is dressed to the nines, or vice versa
E. hoping to get your *own* London Fog back

CHAPTER 5.

So You Lost Your Car Keys

Let's face it, we didn't need Ralph Nader to teach us that the automobile is the most dangerous weapon (next only to our big mouths) in our lives. Equally, our all-American life-style is built on the quick mobility that the automobile gives us. We are bombarded by advertising propaganda telling us which brand to buy, when the truth is they are basically identical and the quality of the serviceman is more important than the name of the manufacturer. (If your Cadillac has an Oldsmobile engine, does your Dodge have a Moped?) So go ahead and read *Consumer Reports,* test drive every make in town, compare prices, have the various warranties translated into English, foreign vs. domestic, weigh the different kinds of financing, haggle about your trade-in and—finally, finally—buy whichever car has a sun roof. Now you've got to get cracking. Get that car ORGANIZED!

What equipment do you need? Over and above the owner's manual, registration insurance and such, you need the following:

A bumper sticker which captures your own personality, like: I FOUND IT (OR, IF YOU'RE JEWISH) I FOUNDED IT

36

. . . I BRAKE FOR ANIMALS . . . CANCER CURES SMOKING . . . SAILORS HAVE MORE FUN . . . I'D RATHER BE SURFING . . . THE ENVIRONMENT—LOVE IT OR LEAVE IT . . . PAUL REVERE SNITCHED . . . HONK IF YOU BELIEVE IN JESUS . . . HONK IF YOU ARE JESUS . . . DON'T CALIFORNICATE WASHINGTON . . . SWINE FLU IS NOT KOSHER . . . MY MOTHER IS A HAPPY COOKER . . . I'M MECHANICALLY INCLINED—I SCREW UP EVERYTHING . . . CAUTION: THIS CAR BRAKES FOR ANTIQUE SHOPS.

Plenty of games to distract the kids on any long trip (anything over five miles is a long trip).

Backpack, plus small camp stove with gas cartridge.

Maps of everywhere, especially South Boston (so you can avoid it) and Philadelphia (ditto). Also it would help if you took a short course in how to fold maps. The inside of your car is a litterbug's delight.

Flares, lanterns and road markers in case of emergency.

A conductor's change-making machine, fully loaded, for exact change booths on the bridges and turnpikes. Get one with a lock!

An emergency potty. And a fire extinguisher, unless you don't have a potty.

Cans of World War II army rations in case of abandonment in a snowdrift or being caught in a riot in Skokie.

A folding plastic poncho (for sudden storms or picnics).

A small refrigerator that plugs into the cigarette lighter, thus providing cold beer and vichyssoise for hot days and desert travel.

At least two extra sets of car keys to avoid the humiliation of losing your keys in Blum's just before closing time and rushing to the car just in time to see it towed away by the traffic bounty hunters.

Foul-weather gear

A pup tent (for your pup)

A folding bicycle

A security blanket

37

You must keep the trunk of the car empty enough to carry the shells, rocks, driftwood, soil samples and pieces of broken glass which your spouse collects at every beach, park, forest or nature trail. These items are picked up in a fever of enthusiasm and placed tenderly in the trunk of the car where, forgotten, they stay until you have to reach in there years later to get the spare tire, cutting your index finger on the broken glass (which your wife insists could be native Indian jewelry but which you recognize as the bottom of a Coke bottle). No matter what the junk, don't throw it away until you get home!

Now that you're organized for safety and comfort, it's time to see to personal growth. You spend countless hours locked into your car, rushing from nowhere to Yennavelt. Why not use those wasted hours to improve yourself? Install a cassette tape recorder and study a foreign language, dictate memos and finish your correspondence or—if you're up to it—meditate on the Long Island Expressway.

It might help to organize your life if you also had a telephone installed in the car. If so, practice talking under water for at least a month because that's what your auto-telephone voice sounds like. Having a phone aboard will allow you to put your "dead time" to work. I can hear you now, stuck bumper to bumper on the New Jersey Turnpike:

YOU: Hello, Ruthie, it's me.

SECY: For ten years I've told you I hate Ruthie. Just Ruth, is that so hard?

YOU: Oh, yes, sorry, Ruth . . . *Come on, move it, you son of a bitch!!*

SECY: You called long distance to abuse me, Mr. Sexist?

YOU: Oh, sorry, no, I'm caught in traffic on the turnpike. UP YOURS, TOO, FELLOW!

SECY: Please, Mr. . . .

YOU: Listen, Ruth. I'm not going to the staff meeting. Tell the boss some lie—tell him my wife was in an accident and got a whiplash.

SECY: Again? I told him that last week!

YOU: Well, those things can repeat on you. Listen, Ruth, what's in the mail?

SECY: Are you calling me from a mine shaft somewhere? Your voice sounds even funnier than usual. Are you speeding while drunk?

YOU: What speeding? I'm sitting here, locked in traffic and it's only 9:00 A.M. What drunk? What's in the mail already?

SECY: I didn't open up yours.

YOU: (distantly) Up yours, too, sister!

Aren't you at least embarrassed that you've arrived at the toll booth—more than once—without a penny on your person? That you've fouled up the exact-change line by arriving in front of a long, hot line and found that you have $.70 but not $.75? It's time you organized yourself for this chore, too. What's the solution? To put the right change in your hot little hand before you even leave home? To keep a change box in the car? Should you plan to go to the exact change booth, or is any booth okay?

Before telling you how to organize yourself for this, we consulted the experts on the psychology of toll-booth behavior. While the literature is sparse, it is also boring, so we went right to the horse's mouth and called upon Dr. Rock Rega, whose office is immediately under the Throgs Neck Bridge.

I asked Rega what are the psychological factors affecting toll-booth behavior.

"Listen," he said, "the first is greed. Some 12 per cent of the people we studied will do anything to avoid paying a toll. We have dozens of subjects who drive thirty miles out of their way to miss the Hutchinson Parkway toll booth. We even had one subject who spent $10.70 each day hiring a private yacht in order to beat a $.75 toll at the Golden Gate Bridge."

"Sounds weird to me," I said. "What kind of person has the right change ready when he approaches the booth?"

"Tight-ass anal," he replied.

"And the one who is fumbling through wallet or purse with all the horns blaring behind?"

"Farblondjet," he said.

"What is that?"

"A technical term, meaning confused and screwed up."

"Well," I persisted, "what else do your studies show?"

"Six per cent of the drivers are self-defeaters. They pull up in the exact-change lane without the right change and/or they pull up so far from the basket that they miss and at least one coin goes spinning down on the pavement while the lights flash, the cops scurry and the horns blow behind him."

"That's a kind of brinkmanship," I said. "I suppose those people like to live dangerously, right?"

"Wrong," he said, "they are commie bastards, unconsciously trying to overthrow the state."

"My heavens!" I exclaimed, "and one more question. How do you *yourself* handle toll booths?"

"Never touch 'em. Why do you think I live *under* the bridge? I take a raft into town, which is cool except that the muggers have now hired frogmen, and an honest citizen doesn't have a chance."

Never mind Dr. Rega. There *are* some commonsensical rules for coping with toll booths, such as:

1. Turn off the ball game on the radio at least one mile before approaching the toll booth. During the World Series of '75, two Bostonians went over the side into the Charles River when Carlton Fisk homered and another totalled the exact change booth. Be cool.

2. No sex within seven minutes of the toll booth. America may be a free society and individual rights are sacred and all that, but there is a time and place for everything. A Rabbit piloted by a horny lecher in Ohio once went into sudden reverse at twenty miles an hour, wiping out a mile-long trail of overheated cars in the heat of passion. (For better organized sex, see Chapter 7.)

3. Remember to roll down the window *before* you try to toss the coins into the basket. If you are a sloppy pitcher, set up a basket at home and practice pitching.

Most people can throw accurately with their left hand even if they are right-handed. However, if you are right-handed and cannot throw well with your left hand, buy a British car, drive on the left side of the booth, have a frontal lobotomy or rent a bionic arm.

Going crazy

If you do not have access to a closet—or if it has been pre-empted by another closet crazy in your family—you can go crazy in your automobile without anyone giving it a second thought. What would be viewed as nuttiness in the real world is excused in automobile drivers so long as we avoid wrapping ourselves around the Empire State Building or totalling a platoon of nuns. When Evel Knievel leaps his car over the Grand Canyon, it's called *daring*. Same with you. If a little old lady cuts you off at the pass, you can have a violent temper tantrum, gun your motor and roar past her, yelling and foaming at the mouth all the while. This is called *aggressive driving*. It may be regarded by fellow passengers as rude or even as overkill (especially if you accidentally kill the old gal), but nobody recognizes it as what it is: CRAZY!

Behind the wheel you can go crazy when the red light doesn't change; when the guy in front of you just sits there after the light flashes green; when a slow truck settles in front of you on a two-lane mountain highway; and especially when the cop pulls you over for a ticket as you hit 75 (in downtown traffic). May the fleas of a thousand camels take up residence in his crotch!

An automobile is always described as a lethal machine, and it is. It is also portable therapy. Driving sublimates more rage and frustration than ten football games or boxing matches. How many mediocre and failed characters derive their self-esteem from zipping about in their sleek and elegant automobiles? For going crazy on the go, the automobile is the greatest invention since the wheel and the woe.

Western man's love affair with the automobile has become ridiculous. We pump billions of dollars into mass transit to cut down on pollution and to lure the auto driver into gleaming new subways . . . and what happens? Nothing. The American driver is connected to his car at the hip, and you would have to sever him at the joint to pry him out of his mad

41

machine. New York City recently eliminated most meters to get rid of autos in midtown, so New Yorkers double-parked or drove around the block all day, smoking fumes and cursing happily.

A metaphor of our time was the California lady who actually left a will instructing her heirs to bury her in her sleek Farrari. They did. And how do you think the good lady died? You're right—in an automobile accident, with a smile on her face.

Back-seat drivers

All drivers must cope with back-seat drivers, who are usually their own mates and sit in the front seat. Back-seat drivers usually offer such helpful hints as: "That's a red light" . . . "Somebody's passing you" . . . "We live in the next block" . . . "Don't hit that old man." If such advice causes you to see red, although the light is green, there are ways to handle the situation. Turn the radio up to top volume. Wear a fur hat with earflaps extended (this is stifling in the summer, but since you have a sun roof it protects against pigeons). Steal a bus sign that says: "It is against the law to talk to the driver while this vehicle is in motion."

Failing all this, gag the sonofabitch and take off in a cloud of smoke.

Keep your car in good repair, and remember that just as a person who serves as his own lawyer has a fool for a client, so a non-expert who thinks he can fix his own transmission is likely to run his car into a basket case. So keep a sheet of lined yellow paper in the glove compartment and make an immediate entry onto the list each time a new ailment appears (in the car). Don't trust to memory—otherwise you will bring the car in for service and forget your chief complaints. If, however, you dutifully inscribe each problem, you'll have a complete list for the mechanic, as follows:

The car does not start in P or N, only R or D. Is this right?
The cigarette lighter pops out of the dash as soon as it gets hot enough to light a cigarette, falling under the

seat. Or should I quit smoking?

The seat belts are snarled like linguini.

If you take your hands off the wheel, the car makes a 90° right-angle turn. Must be something wrong with the balance.

They stole my hub caps again.

Also my aerial, but it's okay because the radio gets nothing but the Mets games which is worse than nothing. Also the radio goes on when the hood is opened.

Everything makes noise except the horn.

Right directional signal points straight up.

Get another set of keys—I'm sick of unlocking the door with a clothes hanger.

Car doesn't start easily in cold weather—anything below 85° is cold by it.

Mechanic told me not to use cheap gas. Ask him where you can *get* cheap gas.

They won't fix these things, of course, because they'll find a much more expensive and mortal problem the moment they open the hood, starting the radio. But your list will look good in a Turkish bath.

Parking

The worst thing about a car is parking it if you live in or around a big city. Some New Yorkers drive around the block all night, waiting for a space to open up, then sleep until 11 A.M. when they have to wake up to move the machine across the street to a Monday, Wednesday and Friday spot. Unless they have the loot to keep their car in a garage, New Yorkers cannot possibly hold down a job and keep a car at the same time. Looking after the car—and shepherding it about to legal spots at various times of the day and night—is a full-time job in itself. It may help to keep you from blowing your top to harass fellow New Yorkers who greedily occupy more precious parking space than absolutely necessary.

43

JUST PLACE THIS REPLICA OF A PARKING TICKET
ON THE OFFENDER'S WINDSHIELD:

CITY _____   STATE _____

TIME _____   MAKE OF AUTO _____

Listen, klutz this is not a ticket, but if it were within my power, you would receive two, and the cops would tow you away to the river. Because of your dim-witted and arrogant way of parking, you have wasted enough room for a 20-mule team, 3 wild elephants, a goat and a platoon of pygmies.

I wish you an early transmission failure (on the expressway during the rush hour). May you lose all your teeth except one, and may that one give you a whopping toothache!

AND NOW TEST YOURSELF

1. When your tire goes flat, you:

   A. do also
   B. know just where the jack is—home in the garage
   C. walk to the nearest Gulf station for help (you have no cash, but you do have a Gulf credit card only because you forgot to tear it up in protest)
   D. change the tire in a jiffy while whistling a merry tune
   E. abandon the car and buy a Moped

2. If you lose your car keys, you:

   A. know exactly where another set is (in your sister-in-law's purse)
   B. what else is new?
   C. tear up the floorboards of the house and also cannibalize the car

44

D. blame the kids and/or your mate

E. also lose your mind

3. When you approach a toll gate, you:

A. have the exact change in your hand

B. first get in the exact-change line and then start searching through your pockets and under the seat of the car

C. forget to unbuckle your safety belt

D. discover you left home without a penny

E. run out of gas

F. ask the collector how he copes with boredom

CHAPTER 6.

Six Undershirts, No Shorts

Right off, we have to teach you how to pack your suitcase. It is a good rule to pack *light,* but it is more important—especially for YOU—to pack *right!* Within the past year alone, your careless packing has resulted in the following totally avoidable hassles:

Arriving in a hotel in St. Louis to find you forgot your kit of toilet articles and it's too late at night even to buy a toothbrush.

Leaving your carry-on Valpack hanging in the airplane in Denver.

Discovering in Memphis that you mistakenly took your wife's matching suitcase instead of the one you packed the night before, and your worldly possessions now consist of a hair blower and 16 super Tampaxes.

Getting ready to go out on the town in Miami with *one* (count it) white loafer, its mate sitting forlornly under your bed at home.

Finding, in Kansas City, you have brought 6 undershirts but *no* shorts, 3 pairs of sox and only the left-leaning half

46

of a pair of tennis sneakers, the wrong bathing suit (from 5 years ago, before you started to waddle) and—unaccountably—an elegantly-laced tuxedo shirt but no tuxedo.

Having thrown everything into the suitcase at the last moment, you failed to cap the shaving cream, and opening the suitcase in Atlanta, you found the entire contents floating in a lather which somehow seemed larger than the suitcase and seemed to rise like the Hyatt House elevator.

Having waited with impatience and jetlag at the carousel in the Los Angeles terminal for the luggage to appear, you accidentally took the wrong suitcase and experienced the embarrassment of being seized at the thigh by a little old lady's umbrella as she shouted, "Stop, thief!"

You are stopped at the airport by a security check when the 5-pound salami in your case shows up in the X-ray machine like a World War II depth charge.

There is no specific art to packing a suitcase, but if it is done with a reasonable amount of organization you can avoid the near-disaster that befell my friend Cheryl, who is a tall version of Mary Hartman, Mary Hartman. Arising at 4:00 A.M., in preparation for an 8:00 A.M. airplane departure, she proceeded (while still in her nightclothes) to hurl her belongings into the battered case her father had carried through World War II. The chore of packing completed, she went about her ablutions when she suddenly remembered—the cat! "Here, pussy, here Ramadan!" Where the hell was he? Cheryl tore through her small apartment, under the bed, into the closets, the dishwasher, the shower. Whoops, the window was open. Hysterical, she raced out onto the Manhattan streets—still in her nightgown—screaming for Ramadan. She stopped the hookers, the muggers, the muggees, drunks, cops, robbers, taxi drivers, "Did you see my pussy?" They all stared at her unblinking. Sobbing and trembling, Cheryl raced home and— you guessed it—heard the cat's meow coming from the packed suitcase. The moral of the story: Don't pack the cat! Make a list the night before and pack slowly and carefully in

47

advance, thus avoiding the kind of NB (nervous breakdown) which Mary Hartman had on the David Susskind show and my friend Cheryl had on 79th Street.

There are certain forgettables which you should always have *pre-packed,* including travel alarm, immersion water heater, instant coffee, teabags, transistor radio, cigarettes and portable backgammon board. Also a damp cloth and a blow-dryer as fist aid against wrinkling (your *clothes,* not *you*). Travel is broadening and joyous, but not if it is done so frenetically that you take off like a blue dart and it lives in your memory as a white blur. You have to prepare and organize with care. Here are some knowledgeable tips:

1. Be sure not to travel to any foreign country that violates democratic principles. This rule has the added virtue of shrinking the globe and thus reducing your options to a more manageable proportion. Right off, you can strike the totalitarian Communist countries off the list. Next you can write off the military dictatorships of Africa and Latin America. Add the Arab sheiks who put a gun to our head in the oil embargo. Now throw in the Third World countries who joined in the United Nations vote equating Zionism with racism. Add the countries (like France) who play footsie with skyjacking terrorists. For good measure, include nations that practice torture and are guilty of repression of free speech. Toss in all those who hate the Yankees (or Mets). Now it is a lot easier to work out an itinerary.

Basically you're down to Canada (but careful about Quebec), Holland, Denmark and Israel. But at least you can enjoy that glow of righteousness which flows from not giving aid and comfort (and good American bucks) to the enemies of freedom. Better a circumscribed itinerary than a guilty conscience.

2. Listen to Karl Malden and convert your cash into traveler's checks, because otherwise you will be rolled in Haiti, stripped clean on the Costa del Sol or wasted in Lebanon . . . all places you should have avoided, anyway, in accordance with Rule 1.

48

3. I don't care how old you are or how embarrassed this will make you, but pin a "Hello, I am ——" identification tag on your outer garment, containing your name, address, blood type, telephone number, religion, destination, seat number, marital condition (precarious) and allergies (small children).

4. Wherever possible, travel with an organized group (a covey of disorganized individuals) so someone else will handle the details of itinerary, luggage, tipping, etc. And you can bug the tour leader whenever you are frustrated. You will, of course, find some kooks and bores in the group who will drive you up the wall, but the alternative is for you to fend for yourself, which means getting stranded at the wrong airport in Milan, after having been ripped off by a taxi driver in Rome, tossed out on the avenue by an arrogant French concierge as you clutch your confirmed reservation in your hot hand, and being taken hostage in Athens by gay Palestinian guerrillas who want to exchange you for Anita Bryant!

5. Eat the local foods. Don't be an ugly American, bearing bottled water and packages of instant coffee and other American-type staples. Let yourself go, open your mouth up to the native cuisine. Remember that in order to live a little, you have to be willing to die a little. And anybody who can eat steak tartare in Chicago ought to be able to eat fried grasshoppers in Djakarta.

Beware the air

In traveling, one of the plagues of modern civilization is having to dry one's hands on an air-blowing machine. It's better not to wash—or to wait for the next bathroom—than to subject oneself to this infernal machine. In winter, you will end up with chapped hands, because who has the patience to stand there, hands outstretched, waiting for the dampness to pass? And what about restrooms in air terminals? How many planes have been missed by long-suffering travelers waiting for the air to change from cold to warm? Better to dry your hands on a hankie or tissue or surreptitiously on your sleeve, than to rub your hands together with mounting frenzy hoping

49

for the dry look to set in. In France and Italy—which you should have avoided under Rule 1—there is a female attendant demanding to be tipped for this indignity. You've got to hand it to them—wetly.

Fly solo

If you must fly, travel alone. Let your spouse, friend or colleague travel separately. The reason for this is not only that the plane may go boom—your automobile could crash even more easily—but because you will meet fascinating people and it is fun talking to strangers.

If you are flying alone, you can live out your fantasies and —for a few hours—assume whatever role tickles your fancy. You can be a Saudi Arabian sheik going to Texas to buy the Alamo; or one of the free-association writers washing America's mouth out with "Soap"; or a gay pygmy swinger; or a Buenos Aires terrorist; or Frank Borman of Eastern Airlines; or an Israeli *kibbutznik;* or a Thai sampan operator. The sky —plus your imagination—is the limit, and your seat partner (strapped in) is a captive audience, especially during the movie. Take along some quick-change disguises, so you can assume a variety of Walter Mitty roles, if that turns you on.

Also, if you have to travel with someone from the office, you may find yourself saddled with a lush who gets as high as the plane and whom you have to carry, along with three pieces of luggage, through two miles of terminals in St. Louis. Or you may find your fellow traveler is one of those sexist airborne Don Juans who thinks his plane ticket gives him a hunting license to chase stewardesses. This you need?

Or—still worse—you might be joined by a practical joker who takes audacious glee in announcing, as you go through the metal detector, that you have an Uzzi machine gun secreted in your Valpack. If the authorities don't give you cardiac arrest in the terminal, you'll get up on the Eastern shuttle and the P.A. system will announce the various fares (military, children, senior citizens, etc.) explaining that the stewardesses will now be coming through the aisles to collect your fares. When they get to your row, your whimsical male friend will throw a paw around your neck and, beaming joyously, roar, "We're on the Family Plan!"

This will throw the stewardess into confusion and you into beet-red embarrassment as all the passengers crane their necks and your friend demands to see the company lawyer and a high-pitched voice comes from the closet of the plane, insisting, "If *they* can do it, *we* can!"

Travel alone. The food is lousy, you saw the movie before, the earplug irritates your ear and the line to the john stretches into first class. But you are free to work, sleep, read, daydream pro or con your neighbor! Free at last, free at last.

The cruise

There is really only one ideal way for you to travel: by ship. Only a cruise can really get you organized. You unpack once and don't have to get antsy again until the cruise is all over. You don't have to decide where to go or when to leave or where to eat and what entertainment to enjoy . . . or what the money exchange is!

You don't have to change your train tickets every other day or get indigestion before you start your dinner from worrying about the size of the escalating tab and how much you must tip. Or be told by a concierge at the King David in Jerusalem in the middle of the night that your hotel reservation cannot be honored, *slichah*, or learn at the Tunis airport that they have overbooked your flight, making it necessary for you and two frustrated Japanese terrorists to seize a cab and rush to the other airport in town. It's all arranged for you.

The cruise is *beaucoup* expensive, but it takes the sweat and hassle out of travel unless, of course, you're prone to seasickness, in which case a cruise would be as much fun for you as a brain tumor. But, minus seasickness, the cruise is the way to go.

Here are the rules for organizing yourself for the cruise:

1. Pay through the nose for a deluxe ship, don't be chintzy. It will cost, but there is nothing to compare to a luxury ship with an elegant bathtub in every cabin, at least one porthole over your bed, elevators to speed you from one deck to an-

other, a good swimming pool, a library, a gym, superior food, and plenty of lonely widows and widowers (depending on what your sex and marital condition happens to be) to fantasize about at least. What with the moon arching the heavens and turning the ship's wake into a shimmering phosphorescent trail, there is nothing more romantic than a voyage at sea. And nothing can become your home away from home as comfortably as a ship, as Jonah learned on his voyage to Nineveh.

2. Get a cruise that stops at the fewest—*not* the most—ports of call. Whereas a luxury cruise is an expensive investment, they really get you by the short ports. The organized tour always looks good on paper, even better in the color film shown on shipboard orientation the day before landing, but in practice it's another bumping in a non-air-conditioned bus to still another ruin, another bunch of shops and another hot walk on seedy streets in a predictable town once assaulted by a pirate named Morgan.

It is at the duty-free shops in primitive, God-forsaken places where your money hemorrhages away (even if it's in traveler's checks, as it should be). By the time your Caribbean cruise is over, all the stops—like San Andrés, San Blas, Cartagena, Cristobal and Montego Bay—will have blurred and become one in your head and you can summon up only one collective vision of a filthy craft market filled with hundreds of identical stalls, all teeming with identical straw bags and coral beads, their impoverished vendors demanding that you "peek," "look," "visit" or "enter" their stalls. The most desperate of them will thrust their babies into your arms, play on your guilt like a violin and urge you to "bring me luck, make my day happy, live and let live, you promised."

Getting back on ship—after being ripped off by your cabdriver who became incarnated as a *guide* with an assistant yet (his cousin) the moment you entered his cab and who stuck to you like Scotch tape as he (and his cousin) guided you into every shop where he got payola out of your hide—is pure joy and relief. So you always look forward to the next port of call, because it seems like a nice change of rhythm, but—watch—you always stumble up the gangplank, straw bags in arms,

52

two hours earlier than necessary, raunchy and hot for the tub. You don't even sign up for the last shore tours; the only thing better than *leaving* the ship for a shore excursion is *not* leaving the ship.

3. Exercise: The food on your luxury ship is probably excellent—in any event, certainly mountainous and simple but lavish. You start with a six-course breakfast, a cup of bouillon is served at 11 A.M. (the super-elegant ships merely fill their swimming pools with it), a seven-course buffet lunch is served out on the top deck beginning at noon and continuing until 4 P.M. tea time. (*Savoir-faire* is eating without dropping a plate despite the French widow stretched out on the deck voluptuously in a white bikini consisting of three bandaids.) Dinner —with red and white wine and champagne (which you recork for another night if you don't empty)—includes as many main courses as you wish to eat, and since in your head you are prorating the cost of the cruise by the value of each meal, you devour everything in sight. At 11 P.M. comes the gala nightcap buffet, which together with the basket of fresh fruit left in your cabin daily, overflows even *your* capacity (and kidneys) by midnight. After the third day at sea you begin to balloon and list to starboard. Since you spend most of the non-eating hours baking in the hot sun, you begin to look like a red-dyed rhino, and the ship staff has to lower you in and out of your chaise longue with the ship's winch. Soon you are too logy and stuffed to walk the stairs but also too round to fit into the elevator (or the bathtub). If you permit yourself to drift into such self-indulgence, you will outgrow your bathing suit and the cruise will become a Titanic for *you*, even if the ship itself escapes all trials.

You must exercise regularly to survive. As the sun rises on the horizon, you must jog the third deck (eighteen full circles equal three miles), after breakfast you must swim the pool and after lunch you must hit the gym or walk the ship from stem to stern. Sex at sea is also good exercise, but the bed—even on the fancy-shmancy ships—is so narrow you can slip a disc or dislocate a kneecap in the process. The tub may be more congenial, although more than one passenger has drowned mysteriously there, and two overfed fellow travelers got stuck in the tub for six days and, far from being embarrassed, had the *chutzpa* to demand a rebate for the meals missed because of their "special circumstances!"

4. Never, *ever* refer to the ship as a "boat." It exposes your amateur standing and is bourgeois.

5. Pick a cruise that stimulates your mind. Great as a cruise is, it will leave you a swollen, burned slab of meat if there is no strong cultural or intellectual component to the voyage. Recently, ship lines have created challenging programs of music, art, archeology, science, literature, history . . . with concerts, lectures and discussions animating every day. This is for *you*. In the first place, it will keep you out of the sun part of the day. Walking to the theater is exercise and while you will probably sleep through most of the lectures—and learn to sleep with your eyes wide open—you can busy yourself for hours on end writing postcards to your culture-vulture friends about your sea-going encounter with such brilliant minds as Saul Padover, Bernard Malamud, John Dean and Andy Warhol.

The cultural events are especially lively when the sea gets rough and the ship rolls and pitches. Then the 270-pound Wagnerian soprano, clutching the piano for dear life, seems to fly through the air like Mary Martin playing Peter Pan and, similarly, the pounding noises of the ship reduce the virtuosity of the celebrated violinist to the chirpy sounds of the village chipmunk.

6. Every cruise is exactly two days longer than it should be. The first few days are filled with the bounce of new discovery —of the ship, the crew (including the identity of the fellow who serves as the all-purpose staff stud for lonely passengers) and your fellow passengers themselves. After a few days, all the blurs begin to come into focus, names begin to connect with faces. By the last two days, alas, you know the faces too well and you circle the dining room three times before finding a table without nudniks, ear-bangers or those mod cruisers who will notice you are wearing an outfit you wore before.

For the same reasons, you are more careful which deck chaise to settle into than the captain is where to drop anchor. In addition, during the last two days the ship's crew—and especially your waiter, the steward and your cabin attendants—begin to go crazy with the advance smell of the end-of-voyage tip. The waiter, who earlier wouldn't give you the time of day, now brings you three of every course, leaps to light your cigarette (you quit days ago) and dusts the carpet before you step on it. Your cabin attendant makes your bed six times a day, whether you are in it or not. The Captain, who could barely conceal his haughty contempt for another batch of spoiled American tourists, presides over the Captain's table, smoking Havanas from every orifice of his body and smiling like a water-logged Jimmy Carter. Keep a low profile on the last two days—hide in an empty cabin on the lowest deck, where the porthole is below the water line and the cabin looks like a Bendix washing machine. And, as you get dressed in that under-water catacomb, you will see a live Indian boy sitting in his canoe, peering in and trying to sell you a mola.

7. Don't call or write home. Your letters and postcards will arrive after you do, and a trans-oceanic telephone call will cost you a big headache and a small fortune, sound like a small child scratching chalk on a blackboard. And having called to see if everything is okay, you will only learn that everything is lousy and there is nothing you can do about it but feel guilty. So forget the folks back home. *You're* Number One, at least as long as you're at sea. Organize yourself for selfishness and self-indulgence. Good-by, world, I'm on a cruise!

Walking

Walking, despite everything, is still our most common form of transportation. It is also still the best exercise.

Walking in the country is one thing; but walking in the modern American city is something else again. You have to learn to walk defensively or you will be run down and crushed like a bug or mugged while waiting for the light to change. So you have to organize yourself even for so automatic-seeming a process as walking. Some rules:

1. Use hand signals for sudden turns. This may seem ridiculous, but I know a woman who made a sudden turn during rush hour at the Times Square subway station and she was trapped between the IRT and the BMT stampedes and was stomped into the counter of the pastry stall. "That's the way the cookie crumbles," mumbled the attendant, gluing her together again and carefully placing her, like a cork, in the surging uptown flow.

2. Maintain a moderate but steady speed. Too fast and you walk up the back of the person in front of you. Too slow and you stall.

3. Carry a walking stick. If you can get an interesting hand-carved stick done by the natives of Colombia, you have it made. This will permit you to feel for potholes on the sidewalks and, at the same time, arm you for any unexpected rape, assault, mugging, pogrom or unwanted solicitation.

4. Also take along a dog. Bigger is better, no matter what Governor Brown says. A vicious-looking Irish retriever (with a sign saying "TRAINED BY THE I.R.A.") at your side will speed you on your way with little molestation, and local Boy Scouts may well lead you across busy streets, especially if you cane passers-by with your walking stick, thus demanding special attention.

5. Walk with a smile pasted on your face and talk to yourself. You may not feel so sunny or find conversing with yourself so stimulating, but in the midst of an urban jungle it is as disarming as a mink coat in hottest Africa. It is inscrutable, stirs wonderment, thus knocking other pedestrians off balance. What do you know that they don't know? What secret pleasure are you savoring? Or is it only gas on the stomach? While there is a slight risk of someone burping you, the greater likelihood is that you will be regarded as another nut and will be given a wide berth so that you can zip along your merry way.

6. Keep your eyes down, looking neither to the right or the left, thus avoiding panhandlers, prostitutes, dog leavings,

muggers and potholes, and—who knows?—you may find a few stray coins or subway tokens among the litter.

AND NOW TEST YOURSELF

1. If your entire family is going to be away from home on vacation for two weeks, you:
    A. tell the police
    B. discontinue the newspaper
    C. discontinue the mail
    D. put up "Beware of Mad Dog" sign
    E. leave a light on so the burglars won't trip and break your television

2. To cope with a sudden headache while on a trip:
    A. you always carry both aspirin and Bufferin and let them race
    B. actually you can't cope
    C. carry a hankie and cry a lot
    D. telephone your shrink, regardless of hour
    E. enjoy being a silent sufferer so long as everyone knows you're suffering

3. When you pick up someone at the airport you:
    A. wait impatiently at the baggage claim while they, with nothing but carry-ons, cool their heels upstairs at the Information window
    B. go to the wrong terminal at the right airport
    C. go to the right terminal at the wrong airport
    D. go to the right terminal and the right airport, but on the wrong day
    E. start with the frantic paging while the plane is still double-parked at the gate

CHAPTER 7.

Organize Your Sex Life:
Think Deep Thoughts

In organizing your sex life, the important thing is not the physical act—are we mere animals?—but, rather, developing one's inner resources, consciousness, imagination and capacity to share tenderness. Great lovers are not physical mechanics or amatory acrobats. They are poets of the spirit, thinkers, dreamers, possessed of fine-tuned sensibility and lusty *joi de vivre*. They are persons whose fantasy lives are rich and vistavision, for whom a great painting or a stirring novel are aphrodisiacs of the body and the soul. The truly sexual man or woman is a whole person, open to life and adventure, not a mere hunter of prey, cutting notches (*buenas noches*) on an invisible belt. Sex is not a score card—let the electricians count up outlets, we cherish relationships. Sex is nothing but the full flowering of the human personality, not some crummy one-upmanship or bedroom brownie points.

So how do you organize for a rich sex life? In this order:

1. Go to museums (American #1 in Paris: "I feel terrible, I haven't yet been able to go to the Louvre." American #2: "Me neither, it must be the water.")

2. Read good books
3. Write some poetry
4. Respect every person as a unique personality, not an object for exploitation or manipulation
5. Think deep thoughts
6. Discipline your passions and restrain your impulses
7. Take cold showers

In other words, to organize your sex life, organize your life. Just as one cannot find happiness by the futile chase of the will-o'-the-wisp of happiness, so it is with sexual fulfillment. It is a by-product of a good and full life, like the prize in a box of Cracker Jacks. When you become a full person, your inner and outer resources developed without too much pollution, everything else will fall into place, although it does help to have a place because the back of a car is really bad news.

YOUR SEX APPEAL QUOTIENT
(TRUE OR FALSE)

1. Impotency is when you cannot make it unless you are on your own side of the bed.
   T_____ F_____
2. Cardiac arrest is when a cop surprises a couple in a parked car in a lover's lane.
   T_____ F_____
3. Compatibility is when the two partners enjoy the same positions on the B-1 bomber, busing, abortion and gay rights.
   T_____ F_____
4. Reading in bed as a prelude to love-making is the surest form of birth control, especially for middle-aged persons.
   T_____ F_____
5. The most frequent time of sexual encounter in America is during the denture paste commercial on

"The Johnny Carson Show." The worst time is after eating herring.

T_____ F_____

6. Playing the radio during love-making is an unconscious denial of sex.

T_____ F_____

7. *Savoir-faire* is the quality that permits love-makers to carry on while the telephone is ringing to tell them the house is burning down.

T_____ F_____

8. The Mile High Club applies to those who get high breaking the sound boom.

T_____ F_____

9. The greatest cause of slipped discs is twin beds.

T_____ F_____

10. A paramour is a lawn mower with electricity.

T_____ F_____

11. Funky sex is making love with the television set off.

T_____ F_____

12. Group sex is when a staff committee screws you.

T_____ F_____

13. Nymphomania is an illness which men spend a lifetime trying to catch.

T_____ F_____

14. Abstinence makes the heart grow fonder.

T_____ F_____

15. I finally got my act together, but I forgot where I put it.

T_____ F_____

HOW TO ORGANIZE YOUR SEX APPEAL

Sex appeal doesn't just happen. You are not born with it. You cannot buy it. You do not inherit it. Wishing won't make it so. You have to develop it, organize it, cherish it and abuse it.

60

How? Watch television, which markets the stuff like OPEC hawks oil!

Firstly, by your clothes. If you are a woman, you should wear Teflon, non-stick underwear and Leggs. If you are a man, wear Brute, English leather or nothing at all.

Secondly, by your hair. If you are a woman, it should be bouffant and blonde and smell of lilacs. If you are a man, it should not be wet or beaded—unless you are an Indian—it should smell like Pete Rose and it should make heads turn as fast as when O. J. Simpson runs through the air terminal.

Thirdly, in your smile. If you are a woman, you smile tentatively like the middle-aged woman who sits in a canoe with her husband in the middle of the lake and gives advice about constipation. If you are a man, you should smile triumphantly like the guy with dentures who bit into an apple unsuccessfully but succeeded in gumming it to death anyway.

Fourthly, by your automobile. Depending on the brand, you will either slink like a lioness, purr like a cat, smell like a rose or your motor will race like a hot rod with a tiger in its tank.

Fifthly, by your personal products. Regardless of age, sexiness comes by the pill (Geritol), the cigar you chew on (Muriel is always hot to trot), the cigarette you smoke (Tiparello will travel around the room like a joint), the wine you drink (your mate will flip if you mispronounce the wine like a big dummy, but Dry Sack will get you in the sack with Frank Gifford), the toothpaste you use (Jimmy Carter says he used six hundred tubes in the campaign), the soft drink you imbibe (Pepsi turns on the young generation, but Dr. Pepper ignites a whole chorus line) and the Noxzema shaving cream you use ("take it *all* off"), not to mention the jockey shorts you wear regardless of sex.

Mistressing

The latest thing is not to knock yourself out with encounter groups or for you and your mate to sit up in bed together reading *The Joy of Sex* (while one mate dozes off and the other gets a crick in the neck). The latest—modish—thing is to get a mistress or to become someone else's mistress.

Not long ago, only the wealthy and the decadent got involved in such clandestine alliances. The pattern was for an aging and rich businessman, experiencing the male menopause that refreshes, to install a young thing in a lush apartment in town and surround her with hot furs and tender embraces. That was *then*. Nowadays, it is different. Now you can do it for love, even if you're a lower middle-class, blue-collar ethnic in the suburbs, whatever your sex, color or previous condition of servitude, and you can find a partner one stop from you on the commuter line.

Mistressing is the second oldest profession in the world. Feminist legend has it that Adam's first wife was actually Lilith and, when he couldn't hack it with her, he said, "This is an age of transition" and took a mistress named Eve. Be that as it may, mistressing has been co-existent with all of human history. Unlike the concubine (who served the sexual needs of the master as a member of the household, and also helped with the cleaning) and the prostitute (who was available to every guy for a price), the mistress was "kept" (at a distance) as the special lover of a given man (usually married) who maintained her in a convenient pad over a sustained period in exchange for her intermittent favors.

All that has now gone bananas in our age of lightning sexual revolution. In our culture, sexual freedom has reached new and hairy heights. Nowadays any adult—male, female or in between—can be a mistress. Thus, mistressing is no longer a mysterious and scandalous role. Who cares what consenting adults are up to so long as they don't block traffic and scare the horses? So one no longer has to be wealthy or male or secretive to organize such a liaison. After all, women's liberation has given women entree to jobs and independent means, so who needs sexist largesse, thank you? Some are rich enough to be called paramours!

Therefore, mistressing—once reserved for the actress and the dancer and the mysterious ladies of the night—has virtually become an avocation, being practiced (because practice makes perfect) by housewives, plumbers, congressmen, secretaries, editors, conductors, politicians, sanitation workers and poets. Indeed, anyone who wants to enrich his or her sexual-romantic diet can get into the act.

Nowadays one doesn't install a mate in a pad (installation charge: $25). The partner already probably *has* a pad. Filthy lucre plays no role. Mutuality and equality are the ticket, and sexual love (or at least affection) is the heart of the relationship. Flowers, liquor, a Bic, small gifts—nothing more expensive than an electric blanket—are acceptable both ways. There are no strings attached and no guilt-edged warranties. It's a mutual-security pact, and if one partner wants out, the habit is kicked. Nor is there any claim of exclusivity either way, particularly since both partners may well be married to two other people living one or two stops down the commuter line, and one—or maybe both—of *them* may know of the arrangement and find it peachy all around. In rare cases, all four of them celebrate birthdays together. Everybody is modern and civilized.

But, you may well ask, what sense does it all make? If Harriet isn't happy with her husband, Max, why doesn't she just dump him instead of keeping Dave as her occasional lover? After all, divorce is now as unremarkable as the common cold. That's the strange thing about it. It's because of *Dave* that Harriet is able to live with *Max* with tolerable contentment, and Dave and Harriet cherish each other in their candlelighted romance but would destroy each other if they were married to each other and had to go to PTA meetings and give each other enemas. Cynical as it all certainly is, a solid affair can sometimes do more to rev up a tepid marriage than ten marriage encounter groups (which, incidentally, is where most affairs start up).

So, if you want to organize an affair and find yourself a mistress/lover (look, the decision is *yours,* we do not take moral responsibility, we're only technicians—like psychiatrists —to show you how to proceed if you have decided freely and of your own volition), here's the *modus operandi*. Read the signals.

You are out of town and you call on a customer. The boss asks you to go out to lunch with his chief buyer. Turns out she is a smashing, well turned out, dynamite and class woman. Lunch is a delight and you linger over coffee and cigarettes. She seems to be as joyous and kittenish in your company as you are in hers, both of you purring contentedly. So, you try to read the signals she is transmitting.

"Tell me," she says. "Who are you really?"

"I'm a salesman. I thought Mr. Victor told you."

"No, no," she smiles coyly, if not archly, "not your title. I don't put people in boxes. Who are you *really?* What *moves* you? Where are you coming from?"

"Cleveland," you reply.

"Oh, of course, that, but I mean—are you *happy?* Do you wake up in the morning and say, 'Is this all there is to life?' Do you feel you are fully alive or just treading water? Are you overqualified for living? Do you think life is absurd? Do you live out your fantasies? Have you known true joy, genuine fulfillment? Complete happiness? Whatever?"

"To tell the truth, our new line makes me happy," you confess.

"No, not to talk business. I'm talking *life.* I'm reaching out to you. I sense some kindred spirit in us waiting to fight loose. I have an intuition about you. You *need.* I can just sense it, I feel it. You *need,*" she stresses.

"Yes, I need my hand, which you are squeezing, to stir my sugar."

She seems lovelier than any woman you had ever known, eyes sparkling and smiling. You sense you are striking a vulnerable and well-protected inner spark in her soul.

"I feel a rapport with you," she says. "We just met, but I feel somehow we are old friends, comfortable, connected, do you know what I mean?"

"Maybe we met in a previous incarnation," you offer. "According to my tara cards, this is my sixth go-round."

"Are you married?" she asks.

"No, are you?"

"Of course, but I don't work at it."

All right, already, you now read the message that is ringing out loud and clear. You light a cigarette and fix her with your piercing eyes, hoping that they don't look watery and blood-shot. "Look," you say softly, "we're too old to play games. We are not children. I'm sure you find me as attractive as I find you. It's the last third of the twentieth century, you know, and we live by the ethic of fulfillment, so what do you say? Think of how much we could give each other."

She stares at you, her eyes wide and sultry. "What *give?*" she gulps.

"Look," you murmur, exhaling, your breath coming in short pants. "You can have me. I'll be your male mistress. You can drop in whenever you want—you don't even have to call first and I don't care about flowers and cards and other guys, and you don't have to call and just say hello and I'll *never, never* call you at home. Believe me, I'll never do anything to jeopardize your marriage. I'll be a pussy cat, purring on the rug ready for you anytime you come over. And, believe me, I wouldn't bug you about how much time you give me. If you have only five minutes—say you're double-parked—fine. Whatever!"

She fixes you with a long, searching look, packs her purse and gets up. "Listen, buster, I don't know where you're coming from. I thought you could be a non-sexist friend, but you not only did not *gain a mistress,* you just lost your best account!"

Actually, you're not cut out to have or to hold a mistress or to be one either. You're cuddly, but not yet well enough organized. You'd forget which stop on the commuter line it is. You'd buy a ten-trip ticket and lose it before it was punched once. You'd never be able to make up excuses. You'd end up cheating on your mistress to take your wife out to the PTA meeting. You'd forget to call, to send roses or poems. The best thing for you to do is to rent a secret pad in town (or one stop up on the commuter line) which you can use either for secret sleep-over dates with your own spouse or—even better—to watch forbidden football games on television without anyone to bug you to fix the leaking faucet.

Whether mistressing or just playing around or hanging loose, even our sex lives must be organized. In the Fiji Islands, where the natives go on the joyous notion that life is to be enjoyed, gold miners have threatened to strike unless they get a thirty-minute "sex break" in the middle of the day. The union secretary pointed out that the husbands get so worn out by the end of the heavy work day that they cannot fulfill their marital obligations. Bachelors, alas, were not included. "We don't want to overdo this," the union official explained.

Bosh, you say. Sex and organization are antithetical. Sex should be spontaneous, explosive, unprogrammed. Talk about organizing one's sex life is the ultimate indignity. Next you'll have Big Brother monitoring our bedrooms and dictating our sexual pyrotechnics. All true. All true. And yet . . . consider . . .

Married people, too, can organize their sex lives. For example, don't let your sex get stale. Every month or so, the two of you should take a hotel room in town or go to a motel in the mountains. Register under false names. Be clandestine. Pretend you are living dangerously, even recklessly. Bedeck the room with flowers. Have wine brought in by room service. Dine by candlelight. Don't call home to see how the kids are (they are in trouble) and don't call to say hello to your parents (they're not feeling well). Don't try to communicate (why make trouble?). Just have a ball, and then you can take long walks in the woods and swim in the pool in delight.

This is not to say that sex is only satisfying away from home, heaven forfend. With proper organization, you can have fun at home, too. Spontaneity is the key. Remember the lovers (married, though not to each other) in the French movie, *Cousin Cousine,* who spent the entire day at the family reunion happily ensconced behind a locked bedroom door while dozens of relatives flitted about the house doing their things? It takes Gallic courage, but to thine own self be true, etc. So what if a civic association meeting is raging in your living room? Who cares if the youth group is meeting in the den? What difference if your parents are over for their Silver Wedding Anniversary. Or even their Gold! Should the world come to an end because the family clergyman has dropped over to lay a guilt trip on you for not attending worship services? What if the television repairman is disemboweling the tube in the study? Big deal! If the spirit moves you (both), remember that life is short, passion is life, love is transcendent

66

and marital desire is blessed . . . and your bedroom door has a lock.

Upon re-entry, it's best to make no explanations—that's true aplomb. Offer them a Tab or a diet soda, but you can always explain, if you must, it was TM time or you had to take a call from Jimmy Carter. Anyway, don't leave the mere leavings of your time for sexual love. Reserve the prime time for the big ticket. What good does it do to organize your entire world and leave your deepest selves to pick up the pieces?

AND NOW TEST YOURSELF

1. If someone of the opposite sex wants your name and address, you:

    A. hand over your printed card
    B. start looking for a pencil and a scrap of paper
    C. what's your zip again?
    D. say don't call me, I'll call you
    E. freeze

2. You feel sexy:

    A. after a good dinner
    B. before a good dinner
    C. instead of a good dinner
    D. none of the above
    E. all the above and all of the time

3. Sex appeal is:

    A. in the eyes of the beholder
    B. in the lap of the gods
    C. the leap of faith
    D. the luck of the draw
    E. nice, but rich is better

CHAPTER 8.

It Will Cost You $30 to Say Hello

Sooner or later, everyone has to check into a hospital. Hospitals are so expensive that you can utilize them only if you are very poor (hospitals don't turn needy patients away, they only wear them out with forms in dingy waiting rooms), very rich or have medical insurance. If you have medical insurance, it turns out to be cheaper to stay overnight in a palatial hospital (at $200 a day before they even touch you) than to have your wart taken off by a tweezer in the doctor's office. If you do not fit any of these categories and yet must enter a hospital—for, say, appendicitis—you will certainly develop instant hemorrhoids and maybe a heart murmur when they hand you the bill. Our hospitals are the most sophisticated medical factories in the world. They can both cure you and wipe you out in less than twenty-four hours.

Pack Light

You don't have to check in like you're going on a cruise (see Chapter 6). Toilet articles, a radio, some light reading material (8 or 9 ounces is good, especially if you're coming in to have a hernia repaired), slippers and some pictures of your family to inflict upon the nurses. That's all you really need, plus a "Hello, I am_____" tag so they don't lose you or confuse you with some other person arriving for frontal lobotomy.

They'll throw you into a pale-blue gown that ties at the back, and within minutes there will be four aides simultaneously shoving a thermometer into your tail, drawing blood from your arm, measuring your blood pressure and giving you pre-op Preparation H. They will find out when you order your TV set that you are not Harry Lockwood (who is there for a prostate condition and they dunk you in the warm sitz bath three times before realizing your condition is inner ear), but that will not faze anyone and they will tie *their* name tag onto your wrist. Now you can dispense with your own tag. The TV contraption is ingenious. You have a remote control gadget in your bed which can turn on the TV to any program except "Mash" and also rouse the nurses gossiping about Dr. Feldisher in the center of the hall.

Get a good night's sleep (if possible)
It is important to sleep well the night before the operation, so you will not ask too many questions. For example, your hospital proudly calls itself a "teaching hospital" and, having watched the "Sixty Minutes" television exposé of how many surgeons actually delegate the job to assistants and students, you spend the whole night fantasizing darkly that a Cornell sophomore will actually zip you open. If they offer you a sleeping pill, take it. Otherwise, you will struggle hard and—finally—drift off into deep sleep and at 2:00 A.M., a *zoftig* nurse will wrestle you awake and say, "Are you sure you don't want a sleeping pill?" Take it and the moment it takes hold, a young bearded orderly named Abraham will slip into your room, pull the curtains and begin to shave your body with a dull blade until you feel and look like a plucked chicken. "Gee," you'll say, "I feel like Isaac playing to your Abraham." "Dammit," Abraham will reply, "why does *everybody* say that? It's so boring." Abraham will then give you an enema, more out of pique than necessity.

Use your telephone
It is vital to have a telephone because, otherwise, you cannot share with your family at home the hour-by-hour progress you

make in such milestones as the first movement, eliminating, and what you ordered for dinner. Also, you should notify *somebody* on the outside every time you are moved off the floor. Modern hospitals are vast warehouses, and you can easily be misplaced for three days in a sitz bath (terrible for your inner ear), lying in the basement outside the O.T. (operating theater) waiting for the surgeon to be made up, in the shower, at an Israel Bonds luncheon in the auditorium, or out on the sun deck. Hospitals do not permit patients to just go from place to place. You must be inserted into a wheel chair or tied onto a stretcher, and you must be escorted about by a bemused volunteer in peppermint uniform who carries a colored map of the catacombs which connect all the buildings of the hospital. Some days the hospital is short of stretchers, wheel chairs and/or volunteers and on these days you should plan to read a thick book, preferably not *One Flew Over the Cuckoo's Nest* or a novel about sex in the hospital, because the truth is it is very overrated and not covered by Blue Cross.

Give them your medical history
At least three authorities—the admitting person and two wandering doctors—will take your medical history. Why do they want the maiden name of your mother who has been dead for thirty years? Why do they refuse to write down that your grandfather died "in jest?" What difference could it possibly make that you always had a running nose as a little tyke? Why does that ancient Jewish doctor always squeeze your cheek and say "*a gezunt off da keppele?*" Who cares if you have sweaty palms, tennis elbow and what newspaper you read while making a b.m.? And isn't it an impolite question to ask, the day *after* the operation, *what brings you here?*

The roomie match-up
It is truly clever how they decide who rooms together, whether in semiprivate or ward. Believe me, it is not done arbitrarily or randomly. It is done calculatedly by computer after the most rigorous considerations of copability. In the old days each bed was reserved for a certain ailment—so you had heart beds, liver beds, kidney beds, hernia beds, water beds, queen beds, etc. No more. Thanks to the magic of modern

technology, the delicate components of personality and character are put into the mix along with the purely medical ingredients. So, as a result, you now have a hard-of-hearing black nationalist in traction rooming happily with a raving Ku Klux Klanner. Or you can have a sly woman pygmie warrior wounded in the Zaire rooming contentedly with a young baton twirler who lost her baton in a truly astounding accident. The match-ups are vital, and hospitals do a superb job at it. Enduring friendships are often forged in the pain of the hospital room, and the number of homicides over what to watch on television has been reduced to a tolerable number.

Name your trouble

Every hospital worthy of the name now has the most elaborate, technologically advanced and medically perfect scanning and testing machines, including para-mutuel for patients of the horsy set. Odds are placed on you by the computers, and the odds are good that—whatever complaint brought you into the place in the first place—the uncanny machines will detect some new malfunction which is bigger and better. Many a patient has come in with mono and gone home treated for pneumonia, cataracts, a ruptured spleen and the creeping crud. This is because hospitals now treat not a part of the body, but *the whole person.* Doctors get special brownie points for finding the unexpected affliction. It's called a "good pick-up," and a member of the medical fraternity can forget all about your long-standing slipped disc in the flush of the euphoria at discovering a half-busted colon (semicolon) or a growth in the tennis elbow. It's like archeology—the more hidden and inaccessible the finding, the more triumphant the discovery.

The whole thing is a bit like taking your car in for a general checkup. If it has been working fine, that will *not* prevent the mechanics from producing a list of ills both alarming and expensive! So, if you can avoid it, stay on the road and don't ask for trouble!

Family togetherness

Hospitals now go in for the family. Just as Harvard doesn't simply admit a *student* but gains a *family,* so our hospital (Our Lady of the Smiling *Simcha*) wants you to be admitted

with your entire family, go to your room together, pray together, perhaps even give specimens together. (One smart-
aleck family *did* turn in a combined urine specimen and the
machine print-out calmly reported the father has tennis
elbow, the mother is in menopause, the daughter is pregnant
and the son is carrying on with Abraham.)

The trend—as already evident in maternity—is for the mate
to play a part (a bit part, yes, but a *part*) even in the drama
of delivery. Seems it's psychologically healthier and also
fairer. Since the doctor is surrounded by his retinue, consisting of acne-faced student interns from Cornell and adoring
shiny-faced nurses (they adore the Cornell students, hate the
doctors), it is right that the vulnerable naked patient also
have the reassurance of loving allies on his/her side. Ulti-
mately, operations will be shared. Let every member of the
family be wheeled in collectively for Dad's hernia. After all,
they'll be hearing about it for the rest of their lives, so why
not participate? Also, the presence of the entire family has to
demythologize medicine—and it's about time. Unless each
member of the family is also anesthetized (at an average cost
of $200 per person . . . payable in advance), a few will be
awake enough to stand guard and see to it that the hung-over
god surgeon does not fall asleep in mid-operation, turn over
the entire *shtik* to one of the acne faces from Cornell, confuse
your case with the duodenal ulcer coming up next, interrupt
the operation to slide a sterile wet glove under the nurse's
bulging uniform or lose his miniature pocket computer (used
to compute the bill *during* the suture, on the theory that a
stitch in thine saves time) deep in your intestines.

Going home

Your brightest incentive from the moment you are hospi-
talized is clear . . . to go home. What a joy to say good-by to
the staff—which begins stripping the warm bed for the broken hip patient even before you're out of it—and to go home,
shaky but exultant. The joy of being home again, amid famil-
iar surroundings, to be cared for tenderly hand and foot
(depending on your ailment) by those who love you most,
flesh of your flesh, bone of your bone, lasts anywhere from six

to twenty-four hours, depending on circumstances. By the end of the second day the dreary hospital stay begins to be seen through a retrospective tint of nostalgia. By the third day, the cowbell which the kiddies playfully placed at your bedside, insisting you summon them at any hour for any reason, goes unheeded (you could shake it till the cows come home) in the din of daily frenzy which is home.

Pretty soon you hear such distant murmurs as, "Can't he even pick up the telephone which is right on his head?" "Isn't it somebody else's turn to bring him tea?" "What will we do if he drowns in tea?" "Would it hurt him to put on his own sox?" "Is he going to do nothing but sit outside in the sun all day again?" "How long do these things usually take?" "Wouldn't it be good for him to at least walk to the television set to change the channel himself?" "Did he think to make up a will?"

In no time you find members of the family hiding on the roof, in the closet, in a locked bathroom and in the car (parked in the garage) or walking the neighbor's dog. Notwithstanding these little human failings, you yourself become hooked on your convalescence and completely dependent on total care where the hospital would long since have administered a kick in your behind (depending on your ailment). Home care therefore adds anywhere from three to seven days to the length of your convalescence, depending on the dosages of guilt you are able to share with your loved ones, all of whom are now feeling battle fatigue and nervous tension and sleeping fitfully while you (glowing with suntan and vitality) enjoy your necessary twelve hours of restful slumber, awakening only when your hunger pains come two minutes apart.

Visitors

Everyone likes to visit the sick, because it is a good deed and also because it reassures the visitor of his own physical superiority. But you have the upper hand. If the visitor is a bore, you announce after ten minutes, "Well, it's time for my sitz bath (or movement, or nap)," and you take off to watch the ball game in your convalescent bedroom leaving your failing and sinking family to feed the guests, listen to stories of *their* operations, laugh at their scatalogical jokes—"What, and leave show biz?"—and to dispense hospitality throughout an endless afternoon, while you enjoy your delicious convalescence, chuckling over the delightful and witty get well cards you thoughtfully mailed to yourself from the hospital.

AND NOW TEST YOURSELF

1. You have an annual medical checkup:

    A. every seven years
    B. only when your back goes out and they carry you, like a Tinker Toy, to the doc
    C. regularly and always come out A-1 until the bill comes and drives up your blood preasure
    D. each time your tennis elbow flares up

2. When your private physician drops in to say hello at the hospital, you:

    A. are touched by his consideration
    B. are asleep
    C. are unaware that it will cost you thirty dollars a hello
    D. have the presence to bar him at the door as a luxury you can't afford

3. When the clergyman drops in to visit, you:

    A. pray with him
    B. ask him to administer the last rites, it shouldn't be a total loss
    C. ask him to change the channel for you
    D. wonder if *he* will send a bill, too

CHAPTER 9.

Who Lost the Minutes to the Last Meeting?

No matter what kind of work you do, or what kind of communal or civic or religious affairs you get hooked into, the name of the game is: THE MEETING. Sooner or later, it will be your responsibility to arrange the meeting. Never, never go into a meeting without knowing in advance what you want to get out of it (beside yourself). The planning must *precede* the meeting. Winging it, or flying by the seat of your pants, or playing it by ear—this way lies disaster, and some other character who—unlike you, did some homework—will steal the meeting from under your nose.

Scheduling
When and where to meet is much more important than meets the naked eye. Do you want a large audience (body count) or do you want a small group easily manipulated (kitchen cabinet)? If the latter, call the meeting in your kitchen for Sunday afternoon during the football season; Superbowl Sunday is especially potent. This way, a small corporal's guard will sweep in during half time, approve everything and depart without even mussing the room.

75

Organizing the room

Always use a room that is so small that if a few people show, you need to send for extra chairs and overflow into the hallway. Psychologically, this gives an impression of dynamism, whereas this cadre would be swallowed up in the vast sanctuary of the local church or synagogue (anyway, with so many easy exits, they would evaporate before the treasurer's report). Also, in a large room, with seats set up in theater style, people feel like spectators, not participants, and they have a tendency to sit on their hands until their hands fall asleep. There is, of course, the resultant advantage that you folks at the head table can then get away with murder, but some joker may demand to know if a legal quorum is in the house and the jig will be up. Also, if the tables are set up in U-shape conference style, individual participation is encouraged, the democratic process is stimulated and too much democracy will ruin the meeting.

The best procedure is to divide the group into ten round tables, appointing discussion leaders and *rapporteurs* and resource people for each table, then inviting each group to buzz about four or five vacuous questions, thus exhausting their energy in harmless blather so that you and the others in the inner circle can bite the bullet, play hardball and make the necessary decisions for the welfare of the whole body.

Organizing the agenda

If and when you are forced into a genuine business meeting, organize the agenda so that the reports of the bazaar, the raffle, the theater party and the Hawaiian luau come up first, along with the secretary's and treasurer's report. Leave the meaty controversial issues to the very end, knowing that ennui and fatigue will decimate the committee by that hour, and you and your allies will have clear sailing in the wee hours. The fact that this trick was used by the Communists and the Fascists, wearing down their opponents at endless meetings, doesn't mean that you good guys shouldn't adapt it to your purposes, which are both patriotic and enlightened and dedicated to the common weal and woe.

Mastering the jargon

There is a special vernacular that one must master if one is to be an effective honcho at meetings. Here is a glossary of key terms and their real meanings:

"Refer to a subcommittee." (Kill the damn thing.)

"What's the bottom line?" (Stop already; you're talking our ears off.)

"I don't want to repeat what has been said by previous speakers." (I'm now going to *repeat* the previous speakers.)

"Believe me, I have no pride of authorship." (If you put a finger on one word of my resolution, you'll pull back a bloody stump.)

"We must sit down and see where we stand." (Which end is up?)

"He knows how to handle the Board (Like mushrooms—keep them in the dark, water them well and cover them with horse manure.)

"I am not wedded to the language." (Who's screwing whom?)

"I will be brief." (Batten down the hatches.)

"With all due respect to the chairman . . ." (How did that windbag get elected?)

"I think we need some time to disgest this report." (When do we eat?)

"Our committee decided to proceed cautiously with all deliberate speed." (We haven't met yet.)

"Our speaker needs no introduction." (He needs a *conclusion.*)

"Our speaker is world renowned." (His "Who's Who" is five inches long.)

"Let us forego the reading of the minutes." (Minnie Klotz refused to prepare them; says it's a sexist *shtik*, let George do it.)

"We need to hold a conference on apathy." (Nobody will come.)

"I suffer from modesty." (You suffer from terminal stupidity.)

"We should not reinvent the wheel at every meeting." (I'm the Big Wheel here.)

"Nobody could disagree with the *principle* of the resolution." (I hate the whole idea.)

"This is a very grave proposal." (So bury it already.)

"This reflects the overwhelming and vocal opinion of our own grass roots out in the field." (Three letters, two postcards and one obscene telephone call.)

"Where do we go from here?" (The custodian is throwing us out.)

"Nitty gritty." (Money.)

"Nuts and bolts." (Money.)

"*Tachlis.*" (Latin for brass tacks, Hebrew for talk less, English for money.)

"All these high-flown ideals are fine, but we have to be practical." (Sometimes we must rise above principle.)

"We'd like Marvin to chair this committee." (Marvin made the cockamamey suggestion, let him suffer.)

"I'm an expert on this matter." (I read the morning *Times*.)

"I demand a roll-call vote." (My side lost.)

"I appreciate the frank criticism . . ." (Castration without representation.)

"The chair would entertain a motion to adjourn." (The animals are getting restless.)

"I'm just thinking out loud." (Blowing smoke.)

"Brain-storming." (Gum-beating in tandem.)

"We're not afraid of controversy." (We're scared to death of controversy.)

"I will not be swayed by Charlie's arguments." (Don't confuse me with the facts.)

"Our deficit is not all that bad." (Let's take out a group life insurance policy and decide by lot who should jump out the window.)

"We honor Bernard as Man of the Century for his gifts of heart and mind." (Five thou.)

Communications

Once you get into the heart of the agenda, you will be talking about *communication*. No matter where the committee begins or what organization you are or what the subject is called, it will end up blowing smoke about "communication," believe me. Since someone will make himself a hero by making this speech, it may as well be you, and it goes like this:

"Let's face it—make no mistake—our problem is not our deficit, membership, the apathy of our members, et cetera, et cetera. Our problem is *communication*, lack of it. What good does it do for us to make important decisions here and to undertake fine programs? I mean, who *knows* about it? Our grass-roots people do *not* get the message. The public at large does not get the message. Remember what Marshall McLuhan says: the medium *is* the message! I mean, turn on the TV or pick up the newspaper and what do you see? A big story about (here insert rival church, temple, civic association, political party, business firm). Does anyone even know *we* exist? I know we have a newsletter, but Kimberly should forgive me, nothing personal, but I'm sure that it goes right into the circular file because the world at large is not interested in who has the flu and whose kids are getting confirmed or *bar mitzvahed* or engaged, and what dimwit couple is celebrating their eighth anniversary. So, to get to the bottom line, public relations is the name of the game, and communications is where it's at! I think we need a special blue-ribbon (why must it always be blue? Why not a *red*-ribboned committee for a change?) committee to take a deep look at our communication problem and to bring back a report within thirty days."

This speech will win you the chairmanship of the blue-ribbon committee and that leads directly to colitis and/or the chairmanship of the fund-raiser!

Organizing a fund-raising dinner
Sooner or later, it will fall to your lot to be called upon to organize a fund-raising event for some good cause. Most of the good diseases have already been co-opted by comedians. And everyone knows there is good money in poverty. But, whether it is a disease or some other cause, like world hunger, there is nothing like a ten-course banquet to generate funds for its amelioration. So you're elected. What to do?

First, you have to honor somebody, preferably a nondescript embodiment of the *Peter Principle* who has achieved absolutely nothing noteworthy except the accumulation of a lot of money and the capacity to lean on a lot of friends and associates who are similarly situated. So call Ralph and tell him you are honoring him as the "Man of the Century." He will be so ecstatic that he will develop an instant mania for your favorite cause and will not even realize that it will cost him ten thou up front. By evening he will be burning up the wires, lassoing and corraling friends and relatives, golf partners, neighbors and business associates in the most effective kind of fun-raising—*peer to peer*. "Mac, they're honoring me for some social disease, whatever. I don't know what it is, look it up, it's a good disease. Remember I gave you a thou for sickle cell? Okay, I'm putting you down for a table, right?"

Mutual blackmail and charitable back-scratching assures a successful banquet weeks before the rueful guests ever assemble at the Pierre to hear the "fan dancer" who is probably a soggy senator (he costs $3,000) or a TV network commentator ($4,000) who comes perilously close to falling asleep in midpassage of his own speech. But there is a better way, and since it's going to be done sooner or later, why shouldn't you be the Christopher Columbus who charts a new world in the fund-raising circuit? The trick is a non-banquet banquet. Here's how:

You nail Ralph, as before, stroking his ego, and you draft the following letter to his friends for him to sign:

Against my wishes, I have yielded to pressures from leaders of the social disease cause to accept an award as "Man of the Century." As you know, I am a private and modest man and I usually make my gifts generously albeit anonymously (if not posthumously). The leaders want to honor me at a gala banquet at the Pierre. Needless to say, I would expect you to take a table and to put the arm on your friends and associates, just as I have done for you in the past.

But, let's be honest, I know very well that, much as you could not refuse to honor me (I could cut off your best account at the knees), you would also be much happier *not* to have to *shlep* to the Pierre, get into a monkey suit, parking is lousy and kill a good evening you could be playing cards with the boys.

Therefore, I am attaching a blank check. If you and my other friends double the pledge you made for this social disease cause last year, I will be honored indeed, and we will not have to go through the *mishegaas* of a dinner nobody wants and listen to dull speeches from Senator Pill, who has previously asphyxiated the Knights of Columbus, UJA, Sisters of the Blessed *Simcha*, and the Polish Sportsmen's League. Are you with me? Show me already!

Cordially,

Ralph

AND NOW TEST YOURSELF

1. The idea is referred to a subcommittee:

   A. in order to kill it

   B. when the maker of the motion is the chief *nudnik*

   C. because Monday night football starts in ten minutes

   D. because the subcommittee is made up of the president's enemy list

81

2. Too many meetings is:
    A. a form of masochism
    B. a sign of a wasted youth
    C. better than working
    D. a form of capital punishment

3. The ideal meeting:
    A. has not yet occurred
    B. lacks a quorum
    C. has a hot controversy on a substantive issue (who lost the minutes of the last meeting?)
    D. serves good corned beef sandwiches

CHAPTER 10.

Don't Just Do Something—Sit There

To enter politics, it helps to be either crazy or paranoid, although the two are not mutually exclusive, which means you can belong to both parties. Indeed, you must bear two things in mind: 1) Just because you are not paranoid, it doesn't mean that they are *not* out to destroy you. 2) If you are *not* paranoid in modern-day politics, you are *crazy*. So, if you go in, never enter an elevator backward.

Firstly, in considering whether or not to run for public office, sit down and see where you stand. Answer these questions:

	Yes	No	Are you kidding
Are you rich?	—	—	—
Are your friends rich?	—	—	—
Are you ethnic, preferably Italian, black or Polish?	—	—	—
Are you photogenic?	—	—	—
Are you a born-again Christian?	—	—	—
Lots of relatives?	—	—	—
Are they rich?	—	—	—

83

	Yes	No	Are you kidding
Ethnic, at least?	—	—	——
Born in a log cabin you built with your own hands?	—	—	——

If the answers to the above questions are all *yes,* you have one leg up already. Despite recent legislation, which makes it more difficult to auction yourself off piece by piece to the milk industry or Gulf Oil, money is still the mother's milk of politics. In fact, the first question your party moguls will ask is can you raise $10,000 up front to subsidize *other* campaigns for your party. You'll have to pay for television, radio, billboards, buttons, bumper stickers and small folding umbrellas with your name on the spokes. If you lose, you'll be in hock up to your ears because nothing—except stale fish—is less appetizing than a dead candidate.

It is important to be an ethnic (or a born-again Christian) because WASP is out and exotic is in in America! If you are lucky enough, like the late Fiorello LaGuardia, to be of Italian ancestry with a mastery of Yiddish, you're way ahead before you start.

But, as Carter recently showed us, the key is *organizing.* Every person in your district must be on a 3 by 5 card. Studies show that winners all used 3 by 5 cards while losers stuffed notes in their wallets or purses. Every town must be organized. Every private home must be a potential site for a coffee klatsch. Every relative must be on the telephone bank. Every month you'll need another poll to guide you on the issues so you can waffle and press the flesh and finesse all the way to the election.

You'll also need one campaign speech which should pop, snap and crackle and end in ten minutes—and it should lace together such words as integrity, sincerity, conviction, priorities, honesty, faith, civility, God, hope, confidence and God (a little divine repetition doesn't hurt).

The media will either make you or break you. In using TV, stay away from talk and interview shows where equal-time regulations compel the producers to put your opponent on, too. She'll demolish you. Instead, buy time and use the extraordinary technique that Mayor Jeeter used so effectively to get elected mayor of Fernwood, Ohio. Just say, "You voters have heard enough malarkey, baloney and cheap talk from politicians. We Americans are smart enough to look into a candidate's eyes and see if he or she is sincere or not, for *real* or phony as a three-dollar bill. So I'll just sit here silently and quietly and you sit there and study me and judge whether I'm your man or not." Just sit there silently, a gleam of sincerity in your blood-shot eyes and a warm smile on your lips despite a fly on your forehead. They'll love you, they'll elect you, and you'll go to Washington in triumph and will never be heard from again.

Before such a calamity befalls you, why are you thinking of running anyway? If to impress your friends, forget it. The public ranks congressmen somewhat lower than sanitation men in public esteem, but probably a little higher than pornographers, garter snakes, columnists and revenue agents. Are you dreaming of traveling around the world on free junkets in the company of a government-sponsored nymphomaniac who types like a beaver? Forget it. The cannibalistic press serves up erring freshmen representatives for breakfast with relish. Want to get up on the Hill and await the visit of a South Korean cotton merchant who will pass you an envelope brimming over with cash campaign contributions? No way. Investigating committees of the Justice Department are feasting on filet de Seoul and—with your luck—the Koreans would bring you a free ticket to a Moonies retreat in Virginia.

So what for? Is it to serve your country? Laudable, indeed —nay, touching. But—should you win—you'll find that you're really serving Tip O'Neil, you'll spend most of your time answering mail from cranky constituents who want you to unsnarl their social security or carry a flag to the American Legion; you will vote on bills you have not even read; you will weigh your mail rather than its contents; you will be ashamed to see constituents in your office which is a small closet in the basement of the Russell House Office Building; you will speak only when spoken to by the aged moguls; the closest you will get to the President is your television set; you will take six months to learn the quorum bells and how to use the congressional subway; and your chief concern after that time will be re-election.

Fortunately for you, you'll luck out. You'll lose. To make absolutely certain of that, organize yourself for the following:

1. Tell the truth *at all times*. The press will love you and destroy you, and the people will distrust you.

2. Reveal every nickel of your meager financial resources, including bank balances, debts to your brother-in-law, etc. The public deep down has contempt for poor shnooks, awed respect for the super wealthy: "Rockefeller stinks, but why would he steal?"

3. Take clear stands on every great issue from abortion to busing to gay rights and welfare. They'll say, "He's a stand-up politician who shoots from the lip," and then they'll bury you in a special place of honor alongside Romney, McGovern, Reagan, Stevenson, Wallace, Udall and Dole.

4. Say everything you know about everything. Their eyes will glaze over and they'll go home to applaud your opponent in his bland thirty-second commercial paying tribute to his mother!

5. Be candid enough to indicate the godawful complexity of some issues and be honest enough to admit you don't know all the answers and that you have not yet made a judgment (pronounced, as by Gerald Ford, "judgament") on some issues. They'll mark you down as a dumb dingaling who doesn't know which end is up. They'll prefer your opponent who boils down the whole can of worms of Middle East policy by saying, "I will go to Jerusalem," or "We're No. 1."

6. Tell them you are a man of principle (especially if you're weak on the facts) and your first principle is expediency.

Thus carefully organized, you'll lose gracefully and you can find obscurity without ever leaving home.

AND NOW TEST YOURSELF

1. Most people feel that politicians are:

   A. on the make
   B. on the take
   C. out on the lake
   D. looking for a break
   E. politicking at a wake

2. A well-organized politician always:

   A. keeps his fences mended
   B. uses 3 by 5 cards
   C. knows which side his butt is breaded on
   D. votes his constituency, not his conscience (if
      you want a message, go to Western Union)

3. Politics is:

   A. the art of the possible
   B. a form of euthanasia
   C. about youth in Europe you say nothing?
   D. an incurable disease
   E. a continuation of war by verbal means

CHAPTER 11.

Six Golden Rules

1. Remember the Allen Rule, which says "It's a hell of a lot easier to get *into* something than *out* of it."

On the public level, the Vietnam war was a conspicuous example. This also explains why Eisenhower was a tolerable President. The bland leading the bland. Ike's predisposition was to do nothing, even when his hyper Secretary of State Dulles wanted to rattle the nukes to keep the Commies on their toes. Contrariwise, Johnson—who could have been a great President—defied Allen's law by believing that American omnipotence could tame every problem at home and abroad. He disappeared into the quirky quagmire of Vietnam. It was easy to get in, but impossible to get *out!*

Allen's law works in our personal life, too. For example, you get it into your head that you can save your best friends' marriage when it suddenly comes apart at the seams. You can't just sit there doing nothing, can you? So you start round-the-clock marriage counselling with each partner, oblivious to the fact that this is a professional task that can be done only by an experienced pro, himself no doubt the beneficiary of a failed marriage. Within a week, your friends' shaky marriage has gone from bad to worse, and you have become the lightning rod for all their pent-up furies. This you figure is par for the course, and nothing is too much to give to your friends in order to save their marriage.

In two weeks, your life has become a horror. The husband calls you in the middle of the night, threatening suicide and/or murder. You stop him. The wife calls from the airport at 6:00 A.M. to say she is en route to Reno unless you care enough to stop her at the runway. You leap into your car to rush to the airport to turn off her engine, but of course you are locked into a monster traffic jam and your car is totalled by a Moped.

By this time, you are in so deep there is no turning back, even though you now have seen the inner nature of both your friends with such clarity that you sympathize with each of them in their determination to split. Their marriage no longer can be saved, it is clear, and you now think it is not even worth saving.

What's more, your own marriage is now going up the flue as your mate has concluded, "How come you don't put as much of *yourself* into *our* shaky marriage as you are pouring into *their* hopeless marriage?" Next time, you'll organize your energies better by remembering the Allen Rule.

Another example: You never know whether to smile at people or not because, being near-sighted, you live in constant fear that you'll look right past your own sister-in-law or, over-compensating, turning a big beaming smile on a stranger who will turn out to be the neighborhood hooker. It's safer not to get into a situation you can't get out of. So wear dark glasses and look downward as you walk.

2. *Be smooth; avoid jerking*

Think back on the many troubles you've had in recent years, and let's analyze them to see how, if at all, they could have been avoided.

Here are some of the highlights:

A. You were working in the garden, walking along the primrose path, when you reached down *suddenly to* avoid a thorn. Result: you threw your lumbar out of whack and had to be flat on your back for six days (arising, miraculously, like from Lourdes, the day after the World Series concluded).

B. You were riding your bike in the village when you *suddenly* remembered you had to mail a letter. Result: you slammed on your brakes so fast you tumbled head over heels right into the Salvation Army's old clothes thingamagig.

C. You were reading the paper in the subway when you *suddenly* decided to get off at an earlier stop. Result: half of the subway door (only one half of the subway door works) slammed on your neck and two transit authority policemen had to pry you out with a blow torch and a crowbar, leaving your neck scalloped for life.

D. You were at a ritzy banquet at the Fairmount when you *suddenly* decided that if you listened to one more minute of speechifying, you would start screaming. Result: you got up so *suddenly*, eying the exit, that you tripped over your slumbering neighbor at table 18, pulled the tablecloth off the table, spilled hot coffee on the invoking clergyman and stopped the maddened speaker in mid-flight.

E. You were sawing a tree for firewood, and you got down to the last half inch before you ran out of patience. So you *suddenly* decided to throw the branch on the ground and break it in half by stomping on it. Result: one half conked you on the knee, knocking out your patellar reflex, and the other half crashed through the picture window of your living room and totaled your oldest son, who should be ashamed to let his middle-aged father do physical chores.

What do these disasters have in common? Simple: the *suddenness*, the impulsivity of your actions. Obviously, when you act jerkily you behave like a jerk. That way lies ruin.

The solution is obvious: Count to ten not only when you are angry, but also when you are just moseying along. Count to ten *before* you lift anything, say anything, buy anything or do anything. Don't do anything sudden. Stay cool; be smooth. Serenity does not just emerge in a personality; it must be worked on, cultivated, sculpted. Whistle a merry tune. Keep your head high and smile knowingly to yourself. For you, counting to ten is perfect—anything higher and you would have to take off your shoes!

3. People

Callous as it sounds, just as you must learn to throw old things away, you also must learn to throw *people* away. Even as your shiny green pre-World War II silk suit had to be discarded because times and styles changed—not to mention the fact that you've gotten so much thicker, it now looks like you were poured into it—so it is with some old friends and associates. People grow at different paces. Maybe some of your childhood friends have just kept growing and developing and breaking through to new interests and fresh creativity. Get rid of them. Since you have rusted on your laurels and your ideas ossified at the age of thirty, these old relationships have now grown asymmetrical. Or, contrariwise, there was your childhood buddy—Buddy—who as a lad used to stand on the corner in front of the drugstore, kicking pebbles, watching the girls go by and whining, "Sheet, what's there to do?" Well, Buddy is now bald and paunchy and a father many times over, and he's still doing exactly the same routine, only now he does it in front of the boob tube. One person's stability is another person's dying in slow motion.

So how come Buddy is still your buddy? Answer: because you don't have the gumption to cut your losses, refresh your friendships, recycle relationships in favor of those that are enriching, challenging and growing. It is true you recently stood with Buddy in front of the TV and told him you thought you had outgrown him, and he whined, "You can't leave me—what would I do with my time?" So you stayed, and that's the story of your life. You're not only drowning in obsolete material things, but you're also bottled up in human relationships that lost their carbonation and went flat ages ago.

4. Anticipate—don't just let things happen

Do you realize that you spend your life *reacting* to people and situations rather than forging your *own* course? You respond to crises (and in *your* life they occur every hour), but you don't *anticipate*. Your thinking is short-term and immediate; you improvise but you have *not* developed the habit of thinking ahead like a good linebacker. It's not too late to reorient yourself, but you're burning daylight and it's time to get on the stick! After all, you don't have to reinvent the wheel each day!

Don't just *react* to the immediate. Think like a chess player . . . 2, 3 or 10 moves ahead. If you're going out to the bank, think of other errands you can consolidate into one parking hassle. How about dropping off that toaster which burns one side of the bread while leaving the flip side virginal? How about buying some stamps; why wait until the last possible night of facing the overdue monthly bills and then finding no stamps in the house? (And please don't just tuck them in the glove compartment of the car where one hundred Nixon stamps are still pasted to the roof; put them where they belong, which is where again?) Do we need milk? Butter? Are the clothes ready at the cleaners? (Check the claim checks first—they already wonder about you at the cleaners since you usually sweep in either two days early or sixty days late and usually two minutes before closing time and without your ticket!)

In interpersonal relations, it's even *more* vital to anticipate. For example, bumping into an old friend, don't ask how her kids are unless you want to make an accounting of your own kids, which is doubtful. It's no good saying, "Look, they are not *ours!* They are grown up, adult, on their own and if you want to know how they are, ask them!" That won't wash, because it means one of the kids was wiped out in a drug bust, one just came out of the closet and another—only twenty-three—is into his third wife, all without benefit of clergy. And don't ask the old friend about his spouse either, because he has probably used up two or three since you last met.

Or take a more significant illustration. One of your office

colleagues is high on the pecking order but a colossal bore in his own right. He invites you to a dinner party. It will probably be as exciting as a PTA meeting, but since he is nothing if not persistent, if you plead business and ask for a raincheck, he'll cash it in within a month. So why not get it over with? Aha, not so simple. If you go, you'll have to reciprocate the invitation; you can't be a taker and never a giver. So already we're talking about *two* dull evenings—not one—and will that be the end of it? Hardly. If you examine your social calendar, you'll find several such dutiful relationships which have stubbornly and wearily stretched over a period of twenty years because once you started the mutual merry-go-round, you never know how to climb down without guilt. So you stay up there on the plastic horse, periodically enraged, developing a close friendship with someone you want to spend time with about as much as you would like to buddy-buddy Idi Amin. Most friendships are greased by inertia and fueled by obligation.

Instead, take the initiative. Seek out people you and your spouse feel you want to get to know, want to relate to, think you would enjoy traveling with (but, for gosh sakes, *don't—* being fellow travelers for an extended period can put all but the rarest friends at each other's throats by the time they reach Tanglewood!).

Anticipating is also crucial in your organizational life in the community, church, synagogue or civic club. Feeling vaguely guilty at having missed umpteen meetings, you finally go to one. (You don't have a good book to read.) Having been absent so much, you are determined to be *visibly* present, thus earning public brownie points. When the discussion mires down into the usual question of how to meet the deficit, you jump up and say, "Look, it's not the deficit—that's only a symptom—we have to figure out what our *purposes* are, what are our *priorities*, what are we trying to achieve. Then—and only then—will all these money problems come into focus." Applause. You've cut through to the heart of the matter. You've articulated the unspoken premise. You've hit the nail right on the head and, while the applause is still ringing in your ears, you're appointed the chairman of the new committee on Long Range Planning, which means a bunch of wasted evenings of idle moon-shooting and smoke-blowing, signifying nothing.

So why did you open your mouth? If you had to speak out, why not, "Hear, hear!" or "You said a mouthful," or "Move the question." You would have been seen and heard, your name would appear in the minutes and you wouldn't be saddled with a no-win committee. Think first, talk later. It's later than you know and today is the first day of the rest of your life.

Or, say you and your spouse want to go to the theater. Plan ahead! Find out which shows have twofers (two for the price of one). Failing that, send away for tickets well in advance. It is smarter—and healthier—than zooming up to the box office thirty seconds before curtain time, sweaty and tense and finding yourselves sent up in the moon section behind a pole for ten dollars a clip, so upset you can neither enjoy the show nor sleep through it comfortably. On the other hand, don't plan too far ahead because the show will close in your face, you will find yourself in San Antonio on a sudden business trip or you will forget all about it. Not too soon, not too long; just right is perfect.

There are two added dividends in anticipating carefully. Firstly, as in sex (see Chapter 7), anticipation is usually better than consummation (and always cheaper). Poring over Michelin's guides and maps for an oft-delayed trip to Europe is sheer delight. *Going* to Europe is expensive and often a drag. (See Chapter 6.) Savoring plans for a leisurely automobile trip across the country is delicious. Actual travel on the New Jersey Turnpike, with an overheated family and radiator, is a fate worse than debt. In many situations, it is better to anticipate by eager planning than to implement the cockamamey plans.

Vital as anticipation is, you can overdo it. In the end, things never turn out precisely as we anticipate them. The calamities we anticipate usually don't happen—or, if they do, they come in different guises and hit us from the blind side.

5. *Purpose in life*

But, wait, after the gimmicks and devices and rules and guidelines, the bottom-line reality about self-organization is to develop a *sense of purpose in living*. Without real purpose, why bother organizing? If one doesn't know where one is going, then *any* route will get one there. Your routine can be efficient only if your life is meaningful because it's purposeful.

Now your purpose need not be lofty and grand. It can be mundane; it can even be negative. For example, maybe instead of you going crazy, your purpose in life is to *drive your boss crazy*. Some may see this as a perverse and unworthy goal, but they do not know your boss. To drive him crazy, you have to organize your life around this central goal. Study a rerun of the movie classic, *Gaslight,* on the late show and see how Charles Boyer did in Ingrid Bergman. Now adapt what you've learned to your situation. Screw up his mail so urgent letters end up lost in his bottom drawer. Call him daily on his private phone and treat him to three minutes of heavy breathing (simulating passion, not asthma). Cancel his hotel, plane, shrink and restaurant reservations at the last minute. Page him at airports with phantom calls. Put saltpeter in his coffee. Switch the paintings on the walls of his office each week. Arrange for a buxom masseuse, bearing a folding table to arrive at the office while he is conferring with *his* boss. Put his name on the mailing lists for sundry porno outfits. Send nasty memos in his name to his superiors. If you can pull off those dirty tricks, while covering your own tracks, you will fulfill your purpose by driving him bonkers in just a few weeks because he didn't have all that far to go to begin with. But, then, what do you do for an encore?

What you do for an encore is find a *positive* goal for your life beyond mere survival. A good hobby—literature, art, music, civic activity, religion, helping your neighbors, self-help, meditation—will help enrich your life and provide a sense of organization so that you, finally, become the master of your own destiny instead of a human flotsam in the foamy brine.

6. Count your blessings

Remember: Life is not to be measured by its length but by its quality—not by the number of years but by the laughs, joys and spirit it provided. And if you finally get the scrambled fragments of your life pulled together into a coherent unity, you can die in jest with a smile on your face, especially with the knowledge that you were sufficiently organized—and prescient—to have left a superb eulogy (scribbled on the back of an envelope) to lighten the burden of your passing. Even the flat nasal twang of your brother-in-law's metallic voice will not be able completely to dull the eloquence of these luminous and poignant words:

"Four score (Sam, adjust the score to my actual life-span, give or take a couple) years ago Mama and Papa Linden brought forth upon this continent a new person, born in love and nourished in hope, who grew up to be an extraordinary human being. Intelligent—nay, brilliant—he illuminated our path. Large-hearted and generous, he quickened and enriched our lives. Those of us who loved him knew there was less there than meets the eye. When he could not dazzle us with his brilliance, he baffled us with his bullshit. He was never afraid to sit down and decide where he stands.

"To his family, he was a source of joy, a tower of strength, an irrepressible *nudnik* and a rock of Gibraltar. He stretchethed out of his hands to the needy, and he always had a cheery hello for the stranger at the gates. Yea, many people have lived valiantly, but he was absolutely underwhelming. His life was a blessing, and in his death, he made the world a better place. Nay, a giant redwood has fallen in the forest and the conundrum is: Does its fall make a sound if nobody is around to hear it?

"But, above and beyond all other ingredients that went into the alchemy of his magical personality and sterling character was this. He was an *organized* person. When he reached his final bottom line, his papers were in order, his affairs were buttoned up neatly, he had provided for his family by dragging himself into the car in the nick of time, he had canceled his subscription to *Playboy*, auctioned off his monthly commutation ticket, paid his pledge to the UJA, given the kids their allowances and written a farewell note to Ma Bell. He learned to do everything in advance, even dying. Who could be more ready?

"It was not *his* fault that he forgot to sign the will or that the plot of ground—which he had bought by mail order in a special sale—turned out to be located ten miles south of Quito, Ecuador. Nor should we scoff that he asked to be terminally attired in his tennis togs, Adida shoes and white ducks and blue warm-up jacket—with his Spaulding metal racket across his chest.

"Nobody is perfect, but this was an invincible man who dreamed the impossible dreams and who strove for the stars—else what's a heaven for?—and we will not see his like ever again which, we will all agree, will not be one moment too soon."

CHAPTER 12.

The Last Chance Solution:
Pay to Get Organized

After years of striving to get my own house in order, the following blurb seemed verily to *leap* out of the daily paper: "Is it possible that someone can take that mess in your office, your library, your closet, your drawers and turn it into beautiful order? Hedi Messoff says she can, and her new business, 'LET'S GET ORGANIZED' is for disorganized people who have postponed for years putting recipes or books or whatever in order. Ms. Messoff's rates for individuals are $100 a day or $400 a week, or open to negotiation for longer periods. Business rates are slightly higher. She also offers gift certificates for well-heeled people with messy friends. There is no obligation for an appraisal interview."

Skeptical of the pretensions of any other self-styled expert on organization (except myself), I sent my research assistant, Chotzi Baleila, to check this authority out.

Chotzi called Ms. Messoff and she was out, but her answering machine made an appointment for 6:30 A.M. the next day. Chotzi got there on time, but inasmuch as he did not have an alarm clock, he had to lie in bed all night with his eyes open in order to get up on time. "More of my own self-defeating and wheel-spinning perversity," Chotzi told himself, as he hurled into a taxi to get to his appointment, hoping with all his heart that Ms. Messoff would be able to teach him—once and for all—that the shortest distance between two points is not an ellipse.

Ms. Messoff arrived in a lather of excitement at 7:15 A.M. "Sorry to be late," she murmured as she dissolved on a long black couch, "but did you ever try to get parking space in this neighborhood? I live in Brewster, and it takes me exactly one hour and twenty-seven minutes to get to my office, but—dammit—it took me another 30 minutes to park. I could cry." She began to cry.

"About getting organized," Chotzi began.

"Please, don't talk organizing at this time of the morning," she sobbed. "I can't hack that organizing stuff on an empty stomach, I need a cup of coffee and a cigarette."

"Oh, of course," Chotzi murmured, helpfully. "I'll just use the time to make up some little lists."

She gagged slightly and disappeared into a back room to get some coffee which she gulped down in an upright position. She lit a cigarette and composed herself. "Now, then," she smiled. "Is this for fee or just an appraisal interview? The machine told me, but I forget."

"Well, it's just an appraisal," Chotzi said apologetically, "I mean, if it's helpful, the sky's the limit, money's no object, because the cockamamey way I live now I think I'm throwing it all away anyway!"

"I see," she said. "Now let's start from the top. What seems to be the problem?"

"My life," he replied. "My entire life. I have a closet full of recipes, and I've never put them together. I have a basement full of pictures, letters, old newspapers, but I've never assembled them. I have a bedroom so full of books you can't open the door. Where do I start?"

"Throw it all away," she said. "Shred it. What's done is done. You can't organize the past. Cut your losses. We'll start from today. Garbage in and garbage out!"

"I couldn't do that. They're precious to me. How could I put a torch to old letters and family pictures?"

"Then move and leave all that flotsam and jetsam behind.

Tinkering won't help. You can't change by increments. Only radical surgery will work. I'm a communist, you know. Go to the bone."

"Wow!" Chotzi wowed, "You do go right to the heart of the matter. What about my office? I can't get untracked there either."

"There's one sure trick for success at the office," she said. "Be invisible. Be inconspicuous. Disappear into the woodwork. Don't swing for the fences—let the others risk striking out. If you have to get up to the plate, bunt. Don't volunteer for anything. Be part of the furniture, and pretty soon nobody will notice you, and nobody will know whether you're doing anything or not."

"Of course," he said. "I've been trying too hard."

"Right on," she remarked, pouring another cup of coffee. "And how is your sex life?"

"My sex life? What has that to do with my getting organized?"

"Everything," she laughed. "Ever hear of Freud? So tell me, how's your sex life? You getting much lately?"

Chotzi blushed becomingly. "Oh, sure, it's fine, thanks. But my bills—paying my bills—that's a disaster."

"You're avoiding the sex question, kid, let's not resist. Sex requires organization, too, let's not kid ourselves. If your sex life is disorganized, everything falls apart. Speaking of which, are you impotent?"

"No," he said, getting irritated. "Of course I'm not impotent."

"Then what's the trouble? Talk frankly. This is confidential, although these days the walls have ears. The only way to keep a secret is to tell only one person—and then kill him. So what's your sex trouble?"

"There's no trouble, and I didn't come here to talk about my sex life," Chotzi snorted.

"Listen, kid, I didn't drive all the way from Brewster for a free-for-nothing, goddamned appraisal-interview to talk about *recipes*. Are you gay? Is that why you have recipes in the *closet*? Is that it—you're afraid to come out of the closet, so you stuff it full of recipes?"

"Now, look here," he remonstrated, "are you some kind of

nut? I'm here because the newspaper said you could help me get organized. If I wanted sex therapy, I'd go to a touchy-feely expert."

"You don't understand," she said. "Talking about sex doesn't turn *me* on, if that's what you're thinking with your dirty mind. It's just that one's sex life has to be organized, too—when, with whom, groupy or not, funky or not, mirror or no mirror, under what circumstances, with what consequences. They say it's just spontaneous—play it by ear—but that's a bunch of malarkey, do you understand? Are you married, kid?"

"Yes," Chotzi said huffily, stuffing his lists in his pockets and getting ready to escape.

"The nice ones are always married," she muttered. "Do you know what single men of my age are available? Imbeciles, middle-aged infants, misfits, bed-wetters, refugees from massage parlors!"

"Look," Chotzi said comfortingly, "I'm sure you have your problems, but I came here to get some help on *mine*."

"Which is *what* again?" she said, returning to reality. "Oh, yes, you're disorganized, you don't get to appointments on time . . ."

"I get, I get, I got here at 6:30 A.M., it was still dark . . ."

". . . and you lose your lists . . ."

"I don't!"

". . . and you forget your toothbrush and toilet articles when you travel . . ."

"Never! Never! I make a list the night before!"

". . . and you do not get around to buying your subway tokens in advance . . ."

"I buy! I buy!"

". . . and you do not get around to answering letters and you don't pay your bills on time . . ."

"I answer! I pay! It's not . . ."

". . . and you forget to pick up your clothes from the cleaners . . ."

"No, I pick! If anything, I get there a day too early!"

". . . and you wear the same suit to the office for weeks at a time . . ."

"Who said? Every three days a different suit, nice button-down shirt, different tie, the whole *shmeer!* Even my shoes I change!"

She stared at Chotzi. "Then, what's eating you, for Christ's sake?"

"I miss my bus," he admitted sheepishly.

"Oh, you don't plan your time right and by the time you get to the corner your bus is gone, is that it?"

"No, it's my Volkswagen bus. I sold it. And I miss my bus."

"Leave quietly," Ms. Messoff said, "or I'll kill you."

"I'll let myself out," Chotzi said, organizing his departure as he ran to bring me his notes.

CHAPTER 13.

Diary of an ROP
(Recycled, Organized Person)

The author would not be chutzpadik enough to lay this entire trip on you if the efficacy of our advice had not been meticulously pretested. We selected at random (a junior editor at a publishing house, actually) a poorly organized *klutz* (Arnold Klutz, actually) and we set out, chapter by chapter, to put him together like a jigsaw puzzle. Lo and behold, Arnold learned to transcend the chaos of his life—and overnight became a ROP.

Here is the diary of one day in the life of Arnold Klutz after he became a Recycled Organized Person and began functioning every moment at the peak of his effectiveness and productivity.

5:00 A.M.: Up betimes to go out and jog five miles all the while doing my income tax in my head.

6:00 A.M.: Read a little Plutarch, listened to some Bach, read the paper, made lists for today, completed office work and wrote a best seller.

8:00 A.M.: Breakfast, watching "Today" show.

8:30 A.M.: Commuter train where I avoided smokers,

talkers and card players—and settled into comfy seat to listen to *Rigoletto* on my cassette recorder, with ear plug.

9:00 A.M.: Arrived in office and immediately proceeded to dictate 112 letters, draft three memoranda and write a star-spangled article for the company newsletter.

9:15 A.M.: Attended staff meeting, drank three cups of coffee and passed eleven notes to colleagues and received seven in return, including two usable jokes and one bomb.

10:00 A.M.: Telephoned Masha, a top ballerina, and arranged a private matinee for this afternoon.

10:05 A.M.: Edited four manuscripts and wrote preface for one and epilogue for another. Negotiated book contract with Anal Roberts.

10:17 A.M.: Drew up lists for evening and next day.

10:20 A.M.: Calisthenics on the rug.

10:40 A.M.: Coffee break.

11:01 A.M.: Organized *coup d'etat* against the senior editor.

11:07 A.M.: Tried out the new jokes on senior editor to disarm him.

11:18 A.M.: Got on WATTS line and telephoned every regional salesman and got some better jokes while discarding several old ones.

12:00 NOON: Hurried out to two-martini business lunch with kooky author we're trying to pirate away from Doubleday. She is a bi-sexual mechanic who is fine-tuning a book titled *Going Every Which Way*.

2:00 P.M.: A quick visit to the gym for ten laps in the pool, a sauna, a shoeshine, a little squash and some anti-Communist poetry reading in the *shvitz* bath with the editors of *Commentary*.

3:00 P.M.: Met my ballerina in her pad. My opening line wowed her: "*Voolay voos plier avec moi aujourdwe?*" She's got more moves than Earl Monroe.

3:18 P.M.: Back to the office, whistling a merry tune, to

meet with the advertising people. They say they have no budget to promote Abe Piskudnik's book titled *Chrain— Jewish Roots*. I gave Al an offer he can't resist. If that doesn't work, I'll have to use my file about his hanky-panky with the fat artist in the audio-visual room.

3:45 P.M.: Completed work on my new invention (which is a file cabinet which self-destructs after five years).

4:00 P.M.: Fired Smiley Henry from Sales (whose constant good cheer depressed the entire staff).

4:05 P.M.: Went out for some fresh air, feeling great, leaping over buildings.

4:10 P.M.: Organized farewell party for Henry, it shouldn't be too maudlin, ordered inscription for the watch.

4:20 P.M.: Sent flowers to the ballerina. Nice note: "Whether on your toes or on your back, whether being flowered or deflowered, you're marvelous. An anonymous admirer."

4:25 P.M.: Cocktail party for our best-selling author, whose book *Honk If You're Jesus* is at the top of the b.s. (best seller) list.

5:00 P.M.: Pack brief case and leave, smiling warmly and wishing fond good evening by name to every secretary, clerk and assistant in the elevator because one has to know where true power lies in an organization and which side of the butt to bread.

5:01 P.M.: Elevator stuck, took out my yellow-lined pad and whipped off a sparkling three-act play.

5:05 P.M.: Session with shrink, mostly about when will I pay for previous sessions.

6:00 P.M.: Arrive home in time for cocktails from the hand of the total woman dressed in nothing but saran wrap and a nervous smile.

6:10 P.M.: Some funky sex involving mirrors, strobe lights, and African drum beats.

6:30 P.M.: Warm bath and compose a violin concerto, repair the fence, fix the stereo, paint myself into a corner.

7:00 P.M.: Watch Cronkite and mail back the latest book of the Book of the Month.

7:30 P.M.: Retire to the study to ride the bicycle exerciser, while practicing on the concertina and listening to Spanish lessons on the cassette and clipping toenails.

8:00 P.M.: Dinner out at the neighborhood Italian restaurant, jotting down notes on fragments of conversations from other tables for future novel to be entitled *Para-Mutual Betting & Gamboling on the Green.*

9:30 P.M.: Rush, late (earliest I have been late in months) to meeting of the civic association. I raise my hand to second some nutty motion and as soon as the secretary notes my name in her record, I whoosh out through the nearest exit and hightail it home into my speed-reading jacket to read book already open to page 109 and waiting patiently on a reading stand, with a magnifying glass attached for my fading eyes and a bowl of fruit and six-pack of beer on one side and a box of cigars and jujubes on the other.

11:30 P.M.: Telephone calls to the West Coast (remembering the time difference) while constructing kitchen cabinet and butcher-block table.

11:50 P.M.: A little midnight nosh (salami sandwiches, sour pickles, a potato knish, fried clams, yogurt and Lite beer) while entering into diary a fully exploited superproductive day in the life of a Finely Organized Person.

12:00 MIDNIGHT: Thanks to a 100 per cent superproductive day, using every cylinder to capacity without missing a stroke, I *had* a stroke and keeled over from a combination of overheated motor and indigestion and, being a BOP (Badly Organized Person), my wife did not know how to administer the Heimlich Hug and instead *shlepped* me into the car and pushed me into it for insurance purposes (it *should* be a total loss). Maybe she's better organized than I thought.

DATE DUE